17

Talkies®

Visualizing and Verbalizing®

for
Oral Language Comprehension and Expression

Nanci Bell
and
Christy Bonetti

The *Talkies®* program aligns with a theory of cognition, Dual Coding Theory, and through sequential steps brings the nonverbal code of imagery to consciousness. The goal is to engage the individual to consciously create and access mental representations and stimulate his or her awareness of the imagery-language connection. *Talkies®* is not intended to diagnose or be an exclusive treatment for speech-language pathology and audiology disorders.

Illustrations: Phyllis Lindamood

Gander Publishing
412 Higuera Street, Suite 200
San Luis Obispo, CA 93401
805-541-5523 • 800-554-1819

Printed in China.

11 10 09 08 3 4 5 6

ISBN 0-945856-51-2

3-080715

Acknowledgements

Nanci Bell ❧

Special acknowledgements go to all the children and parents who broke my heart, giving me the courage and stamina to go to the keyboard one more time. I am grateful also to my friend Pat Lindamood, whose love and support will last forever; to my son Rodney, who quietly helps through the night; to my daughter Alison, who first used some of these steps years ago with a little boy in Berkeley; to my dear friend Al Paivio, for Dual Coding Theory; to Phyllis Lindamood, for her wit and art; to our editors, Michael Sweeney and Ben Earl, for their talent and patience; to my coauthor Christy Bonetti, for her commitment to our children; and to my friend Ricki Robinson, for passionately connecting me to autism.

Christy Bonetti ❧

Special acknowledgements go to my husband David, and my three children, Taylor, Connor, and Brenen, for their constant support and love. They are my life.

I am grateful to the women in my family who showed me strength, integrity, and humor: Bib, Mom, Nanci, and Anne.

Also, special thanks go to Trisha Suvari for our brain-storming sessions together.

Dedication

To Rhett and Dad

And all the children—the flaming flowers that brightly blaze.

We are listening.

Starry, starry night
Paint your palette blue and gray
Look out on a summer's day
With eyes that know the darkness in my soul.

Shadows on the hills
Sketch the trees and the daffodils
Catch the breeze and the winter chills
In colors on the snowy linen land.

Now I understand
What you tried to say to me
And how you suffered for your sanity
And how you tried to set them free.

They would not listen
They did not know how
Perhaps they'll listen now.

Starry, starry night
Flaming flowers that brightly blaze
Swirling clouds in violet haze.

—excerpted from "Vincent"
by Don McLean,
singer/songwriter, copyright 1971

The Contents

Foreword ix
Preface xi

The Concept

Chapter 1: From a Silent Movie to a Talkie 3
Chapter 2: Dual Coding: Integrating Imagery and Language 5
Chapter 3: *Visualizing and Verbalizing* Meets *Talkies* 9

The Process

Chapter 4: Chip and a Guide 21
Chapter 5: The Climate: A Short What and Why 29
Chapter 6: Sensory-Language Play 33
Chapter 7: Talking Words 51
Chapter 8: Talking Sentences 89
Chapter 9: Simple Picture to Picture 115
Chapter 10: Simple Word Imaging 133
Chapter 11: Simple Sentence Imaging 145
Chapter 12: Talking Picture Stories 155
Chapter 13: Simple Sentence by Sentence 163

The Summary

Chapter 14: Autism and Dual Coding 183
Chapter 15: Who Is a *Talkies* Student? 189
Chapter 16: What Happened to Chip? 195

The Appendix

The Steps 198
Bibliography 225

Talkies

Foreword

The brain can only receive information from our senses, and it is a multisensory organ. National and international neurophysiological research dating from the 1960s indicates the brain wants to network and integrate that multisensory information as it moves it to the frontal cortex for cognitive processing. Also, through sensory-cognitive research, we helped to provide pioneering data on differences that genetics causes for individuals in the conscious awareness of this multisensory information. A portion of the population has been documented as unable to consciously access and integrate certain aspects of this multisensory information. Surprisingly, this is irrespective of gender, general intelligence, socio-economic class, native language, and age.

It is encouraging to report that intervention research reveals establishing sensory-language connections is the key to establishing those aspects of multisensory integration which individuals do not access genetically. The sensory information must be experienced as a physical reality through the "respond to the response" questioning by the instructor and discovery interactions. Language can then label the physical sensory reality which was discovered, and this sensory reality can then be talked about and thought about. On the basis of fifty years of research, brain scientist Karl Pribram (1991) observed that we cannot think about something of which we are not consciously aware, and we cannot be aware of something not perceived sufficiently at the sensory level to come to consciousness. This is why the discovery of the physical sensory reality is so important. If we try to tell someone else a sensory reality we have perceived, they can only memorize our label for it and try to remember it by that auditory label. The physical reality of the sensory information which the label named was not experienced and is still not accessible to the other person. The role of multisensory integration is that the integration of a different source of sensory information can bring the missing source of sensory information to conscious awareness.

For example, a severely dyslexic neurosurgeon was absolutely positive that his tongue made no action in producing the /k/ sound although he could see that my tongue did. After the use of a mirror and flashlight permitted him to see his own tongue act in that same certain way in a specific place to produce that /k/ sound, he put the visual aids down, made the /k/ sound again and said, "Oh! Now I can feel my tongue action as it goes back and up against the top of my mouth!" The integration of seeing with feeling, and the use of language to describe it, verified where he needed to center his attention on his motor-kinesthetic feedback to be more aware of it.

Typical teaching interaction tends to tell information, rather than questioning at the sensory level for discovery and sensory-language connections. Ideally, to change that pattern, the questioning for discovery would be modeled, and then supervised practice given. Supervised practice is obviously the problem when working from a manual, but Nanci and Christy have made it possible for you to do the practice in a "modified" form. Throughout the manual they have provided sample dialogues to model the instructor's questioning for sensory discovery. They have also provided models of responding to error responses in a positive way followed by questioning for self-correction by the student.

It has long been recognized that "Language" has too broad a scope to be considered the purview only of Speech Language Pathologists. This should also be considered the case for implementing the concepts in this *Talkies* Manual. Therapists in disciplines involved in the mental and physical development of individuals from preschool age to adulthood have clients who will benefit from the language imaging procedures described here. The procedures establish the sensory-language connections which are so important.

Pat Lindamood, M.S.,CCC-SLP

February 2006

Preface

While the *Visualizing and Verbalizing for Language Comprehension and Thinking* (*V/V*) program has helped many children, for years we wanted to write a primer to *V/V* for students who were too challenged by the program. Now we have. *Talkies* develops the imagery-language connection for young children, children with weakness in receptive and expressive oral language skills, and children on the autistic spectrum. The goal is to bring the sensory input of imagery to a conscious level and to connect that imagery to language processing.

In putting the steps on paper, an imaginary "you" has appeared once again, ever there to talk to in the early morning hours at the keyboard. This manual is for you. You will read about Chip, a six year old whom we take through the little steps of *Talkies* so you can observe the interaction necessary to develop the dual coding of imagery and language. Chip is moderately impaired in language processing and he has behavioral issues that were not included in the sample lessons. Chip's story is a real story.

Imagery is a physical sensory connection to language. *Talkies* has a pattern of lots of little steps within big steps with the explicit goal of bringing the sensory information of imagery to a conscious level for students. The little steps are purposely repetitive practice. They consistently move through a sequence of receptive practice, expressive practice, and imagery practice.

You represent our hope to make a difference for the many children that need us all to try harder to bring them from darkness to light. While there may be areas of a child's life that we can't change or affect, we can teach them to comprehend and express language. We can teach them to communicate and think critically. This we can do. This you can do.

Nanci Bell and Christy Bonetti

February 2006

The Concept

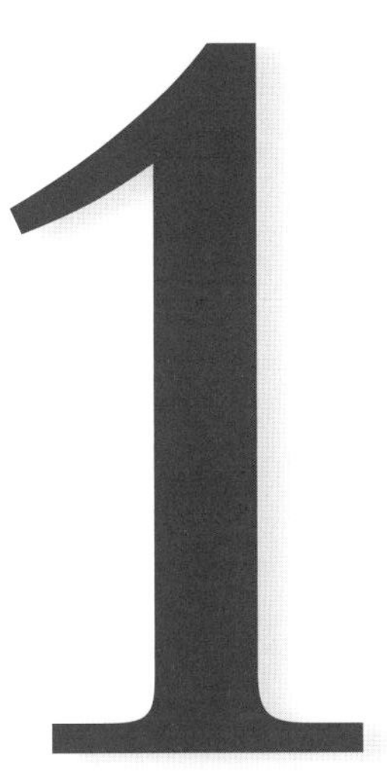

From a Silent Movie to a Talkie

A little boy with dark hair and big brown eyes looked around the room. He gripped his mother's hand while his father reassuringly touched the top of his head. At six years old, Chip had been brought to a new professional to try yet another intervention.

Chip didn't really "talk." He had difficulty understanding and expressing language, causing him to seemingly reside in his own world, surrounded by frustration, anger, and sadness. He rarely laughed—he seemed alone.

A thick file documented years of speech therapy, a variety of professional consultations, and individualized therapy to develop Chip's affect and engagement through play interaction. His history showed delayed language acquisition and a diagnosis of Autism Spectrum Disorder (ASD).

Despite extensive effort and small important successes, at six years old Chip had difficulty communicating his wants and needs with language. Often his frustration grew until either his behavior worsened or he retreated to his aloneness.

As Chip began first grade, his teachers and parents were desperate to help him. He had difficulty interacting with the children in his class, often sitting alone or demonstrating inappropriate behavior that caused the other children to avoid him. He had difficulty making friends and responding to instruction or verbal communication.

Chip stood gazing around my office. As I went forward to greet him, he avoided my eyes, looking at some toys on a nearby table. I searched for clues. Did he make eye contact? What was his body language? How did he interact with his parents? Did he understand basic language concepts? How much and how well did he express himself verbally? What was his behavior? What was the level of his engagement and attention?

With Chip in the comfort of his parents' presence, I began a screening process to determine, as objectively as possible, his strengths and weaknesses. His difficulty receiving and expressing language was soon evident, manifesting itself in his difficulty sustaining attention, rather than the opposite as is often maintained.

As my diagnostic interaction proceeded, Chip often appeared to recede from the situation, moving away from me and his parents, looking randomly at things in the room, emotionally removing himself from his immediate environment and entering into his own world. Sometimes he made eye contact, and sometimes he talked. His expressive language was characterized by short sentences or random words.

As expected, my screening matched the long history in Chip's file. Given that I believe communication and cognitive processing stem from the interaction between sensory information and language, the question was then whether or not we could develop Chip's sensory processing. Could we develop his imagery to a conscious level that would enable him to integrate imagery with language—to dual code? Could we find Chip and bring him into a world largely dependent on communication skills?

We prescribed and initiated a period of intensive intervention, four hours a day, five days a week. Specific steps to integrate imagery and language were introduced and overlapped. The first few weeks used "play" to establish reciprocity, trust, and interaction while at the same time stimulating the integration of imagery with language. The following chapters tell the story of Chip, who in five months went from a figurative silent movie to a "Talkie." As his sensory-language processing developed so did his ability to respond to instruction, directions, and conversation. He began to make friends, contributing verbally in social situations.

As a parent or a teacher, you teach vocabulary and you teach language skills everyday. You can do the *Talkies* program, too. You can do anything.

Dual Coding: Integrating Imagery and Language

Talkies instruction is based on a theoretical model, Dual Coding Theory (DCT). Allan Paivio, a cognitive psychologist, researched and developed DCT as a theoretical model for cognition. He stated, "Cognition is proportional to the extent that the coding mechanisms of mental representations (imogens) and language (logogens) are integrated." He suggested that linguistic competence and performance are based on a substrate of imagery. "Imagery includes not only static representations but also dynamic representations of action sequences and relationships between objects and events."

Our extensive experience in language and literacy instruction verifies Paivio's theory. Imagery is a sensory-cognitive function basic to many types of language processing. As Karl Pribram, a cognitive psychologist, stated, "We cannot think about something of which we are not consciously aware, and we cannot be aware of something not perceived sufficiently at the sensory level to come to consciousness." The role of *Talkies* is to bring the *sensory information of imagery to a conscious level* so it can then be accessed as a sensory tool and integrated with language to establish dual coding.

A Brief History of Imagery and Cognition

Imagery has long been discussed in the cognitive sciences. Aristotle, in his contemplations on the ability to reason, theorized that man cannot think without mental imagery. "Memory or remembering is a state induced by mental images."

Thomas Aquinas, in the 12th century, stated, "Man's mind cannot understand thoughts without images of them." William James (1890) suggested the static meaning of concrete words consists of "sensory images awakened." Piaget wrote, "...Over time schemata become internalized in the form of imaged thought." (Piaget & Inhelder, 1971). The psychologist Edward Titchener wrote, "My mind, in its ordinary operations, is a fairly complete picture gallery, not of finished paintings, but of impressionist notes." Kosslyn (1994), in *Image and Brain*, stated, "For present purposes, all that is important is that imagery relies on topographically organized regions of the cortex, which support depictive representations."

Of the many thoughts on imagery as related to cognition, probably the most illuminating is from Albert Einstein. Einstein's esteemed contributions were the result of his ability to think critically and creatively—and he made his thinking concrete with the sensory-cognitive function of mental imagery. He stated, "If I can't picture it, I can't understand it." This not only illuminates his genius, but also illuminates a truth about thinking and language processing.

The ability to create mental representations is a sensory process that Einstein could easily access, but others cannot. There are individual differences in the vividness and speed of creating and accessing mental imagery. We cannot assume mental imagery ability.

Two Types of Imagery Ability: Parts and Wholes

As noted earlier, extensive experience instructing all ages of individuals became an invaluable source of information regarding the role of imagery as sensory information for language processing. The instructional interaction revealed a parts-whole issue, a two-sided coin, in processing language. Strength or weakness in imagery ability was at the heart of the issue.

Some individuals have a propensity to create and access one type of imagery, while other individuals have a propensity to create and access another type of imagery. One type of imagery is primarily related to one type of language processing, and the other is related to a different type of language processing. The two types of imagery are symbol imagery and concept imagery, the parts and the whole. Symbol imagery processes the parts (letters) and concept imagery processes the whole (gestalt).

Individuals may have a propensity for, or strength in, only one type of imagery. For example, some individuals may have strength in symbol imagery, yet weakness in concept imagery. They decode better than they comprehend. However, the opposite may be true. Some individuals may have strength in concept imagery, yet weakness in symbol imagery. They comprehend better than they decode. Imagery is not just imagery. Strength in symbol imagery does not guarantee strength in concept imagery, and vice versa.

Concept imagery is the ability to create mental representations for a whole, a gestalt. It requires dynamic mental representations that can be rapidly created for color, size, time, space, and action sequences between objects and events. Concept imagery is necessary for language comprehension and expression, critical thinking, problem solving, following directions, and creativity. Einstein accessed his concept imagery when he used an imaged gestalt to problem solve and reason. When concept imagery is fully intact, an individual is able to rapidly create and access mental representations, especially critical for processing oral language that comes and goes quickly in and out of our sensory system.

Symbol imagery is the ability to create mental representations for sounds and letters within words. It is a more static mental representation than concept imagery and is necessary for reading and spelling words. When symbol imagery is fully intact, an individual is able to rapidly create and access mental representations for sounds and letters within words, and words as a whole. This ability translates to strength in phonemic awareness, word attack, word recognition, spelling, paragraph reading accuracy, and contextual reading fluency.

It is important to recognize that imagery, both concept and symbol imagery, is a primary sensory-cognitive domino that needs to be developed and directly applied to language processing. Weakness in processing language often translates to social problems, a weak self-image, frustration, unhappiness, anger, and a host of other problems.

Talkies

3 *Visualizing and Verbalizing* Meets *Talkies*

The *Visualizing and Verbalizing for Language Comprehension and Thinking* (*V/V*) program was developed without knowledge of the theoretical model of dual coding, but it soon became evident that the premise and steps of *V/V* embodied DCT.

The goal of the *V/V* program is to develop concept imagery for oral and written language processing. As noted earlier, some individuals are able to rapidly and automatically create an imaged gestalt from language they hear or language they read. They easily bring parts of language (words, sentences, paragraphs) to a whole and from that imaged gestalt they can comprehend oral language, comprehend what they read, problem solve, think logically, think creatively, "get the big picture," move from concrete to abstract thinking, express themselves relevantly, make their point, get humor, read social situations, make inferences, draw conclusions, and attend to all levels of communication.

This ability to create an imaged gestalt is a basic and primary asset in the sensory system, yet there are many children and many adults who find concept imagery difficult, slow, or unavailable. However, these individuals may visualize parts well, such as facts or details. Rapid imagery of words and sentences is required for concept imagery but it isn't required to process parts, which could explain why individuals with weak concept imagery often appear to be stuck on parts. It is the parts that they are able to image. They can create images for small bits of language—letters, isolated facts, parts of oral language, parts of directions, parts of written language, parts of movies, and parts of social situations. Sometimes the parts seem to be overwhelming and consuming.

In processing oral language, such as in a conversation, the problem caused by primarily grasping parts can be confusing to everyone, including the individual with the disorder. A part of a conversation or lecture is imaged and processed, and then discussed irrelevantly because the point of the conversation may have been missed. The main idea is lost somewhere in an array of random bits and pieces. The critical thinking ability to make an inference or draw a conclusion is impaired by a limited gestalt from which to think and from which to express language. The random and unconnected imaged bits and pieces bounce back in the form of random and unconnected verbal expression lacking sequence and relevance. Parts go in and parts come out.

Social situations often suffer the same fate. Parts of social interaction and communication are grasped, and then often misread and reacted to with negative consequences. Personal interaction is difficult if language is swirling around with a jumble of parts that are processed and expressed.

Symptoms of Weak Concept Imagery

Weakness in concept imagery ranges from mild to severe. Some individuals may experience very moderate difficulty creating imaged gestalts and can compensate by doing something rather easy, like rereading text. However, as the weakness in imaging gestalts becomes more severe, so do the symptoms and the labels, such as hyperlexia and/or ASD.

Individuals with weak concept imagery may have the following symptoms:

- They have a tendency to process parts more than, or rather than, wholes. They get details rather than the big picture and they attend to facts more than concepts.
- They experience difficulty with conceptual, critical, logical, and abstract thinking. They get stuck on details and parts, enjoying facts rather than concepts. They appear to be concrete thinkers because their processing strength is in parts-specific images.
- They have difficulty grasping oral language, whether stories, conversations, or lectures. They don't enjoy or respond to oral language and find it difficult to sustain attention because they miss the point or have experienced unsuccessful interactions. They appear to process irrelevant or incidental parts of what is expressed, sometimes asking and re-asking the same question, and they may be labeled a poor listener or inattentive.

- They have weak reading comprehension. They may have good skills in oral vocabulary and decoding, but words go "in one ear and out the other" when they read. They have difficulty grasping the whole and answering higher order thinking questions such as the main idea, an inference, a conclusion, and a prediction. They often have to read sentences, paragraphs, and chapters more than once and they still may not be successful in answering questions.

- They experience difficulty following oral and written directions. They find themselves confused with more than one or two directions, and language appears to go in and out without being held long enough to process all the directions.

- They experience weakness in verbal expression. Their language expression is often an array of parts, facts, and details that they have imaged, stored, and retrieved. Their language is disconnected and not sequential. Sometimes their verbal expression is repressed, or sometimes it is excessive but scattered and disconnected.

- They experience difficulty in social situations. They are lost in social situations because of their weakness in comprehending and expressing oral language. With weak communication skills, they may make inappropriate comments or exhibit inappropriate behavior, appearing unresponsive to others.

- They have difficulty in written expression. Their writing reflects their parts-thinking. They write in disconnected, unrelated parts and misinterpret the question.

- They have difficulty getting humor. They take language literally and may miss the point of a joke, as they can't see the imagery of the play on words. They may respond to physical humor such as a pie in the face but can't process language-based humor. In trying to fit in socially, they may laugh at inappropriate times.

- They have difficulty reading social situations. They grasp parts of conversations or social interactions, causing them to make inappropriate expressions or actions.

- They have difficulty grasping the concept of cause and effect. Their weakness in processing the whole prevents them from understanding cause and effect relationships that are inherently dependent on comparing a part to a whole.
- They may prefer their own company. If they experience many of the symptoms above, the communicating-world seems to be puzzling, disconcerting, and meaningless, often causing them stress, frustration, and unhappiness.

The Visualizing and Verbalizing Program

Individuals with weakness in forming gestalt images from language cannot just be told to picture language concepts. Concept imagery has to be directly and explicitly developed with specific steps and specific questioning to bring imagery to a level of consciousness as a tool to process language. Beginning with the smallest unit of language, a word, *V/V* extends the imagery-language connection to sentences and paragraphs of language. Here is a brief summary of the sequential *V/V* steps, for which *Talkies* is the primer.

1. Picture to Picture

    The goal of Picture to Picture is to develop fluent, detailed verbalization from a given picture, a prerequisite to developing detailed verbal descriptions of a generated image (the next *V/V* step). The student describes a given picture, using the *structure words*: *what*, *size*, *color*, *number*, *shape*, *where*, *when*, *background*, *movement*, *mood*, *perspective*, and *sound* as concrete descriptive elements to be included in a verbal description. The teacher questions to specifically direct the student's verbalization.

2. Word Imaging

    The goal is to develop detailed visualizing and verbalizing (dual coding) for a single word, a *known noun* that will become the subject of sentence imagery in later steps. The student describes a generated image for a single word, beginning with a personal image and extending to a high-imagery known noun such as *cowboy* or *clown*. The teacher questions to specifically direct the student's imagery.

3. Single Sentence Imaging

   The goal is to continue to extend the imagery and language from one word to a phrase or sentence. The steps are overlapped, enabling the student to use a previously visualized and verbalized known noun as the subject of a sentence. "Keep the clown you just visualized for this sentence: *The clown jumped on the red ball.*" The teacher questions to develop imagery for the words in the high-imagery sentence.

4. Sentence by Sentence Imaging

   The goal is to extend the integration of imagery and language to a gestalt—sentence by sentence. The stimulation begins receptively from a short, self-contained paragraph. The student places a colored square to represent each imaged sentence. At the completion of the sentence by sentence imagery and verbalization, the student gives a sequential *picture summary* to reverbalize the images for each sentence, and then gives a *word summary* to verbally paraphrase the whole.

5. Sentence by Sentence with Higher Order Thinking (HOT)

   The goal is to apply the gestalt imagery (developing in the previous step) to critical thinking. The same sentence by sentence procedure of placing colored squares and sequentially summarizing the imaged-parts toward the whole is extended to processing the main idea, an inference, a conclusion, and a prediction. "What was the main thing you pictured from that paragraph? From all your images, why do you think...?"

6. Multiple Sentence, Paragraph, and Whole Page Imaging with HOT

   The goal of the next steps is to increase and extend the language input, either receptive or expressive, to develop the imaged gestalt and apply that sensory-cognitive base to critical thinking, problem solving, and interpretation.

The steps develop the sensory input of imagery to a conscious level that can be stored, retrieved, and consciously accessed for problem solving, critical thinking, oral and written language comprehension, following directions, play, and interpreting and interacting in social situations (pragmatics).

Visualizing and Verbalizing Meets Talkies

For many years, the *V/V* program has successfully developed receptive and expressive language comprehension/expression, critical thinking, and problem solving in many students. Soon the task of developing symbol imagery for reading and spelling acquisition presented itself, leading to the question as to whether or not dual coding was a widely applicable theoretic model for language and learning. Could imagery be directly and explicitly stimulated, developed, and applied—and the dual coding model adapted—to decoding and encoding skills? Years of clinical and classroom research provided an answer. Yes, conscious development and application of imagery with the *Seeing Stars: Symbol Imagery for Phonemic Awareness, Sight Words, and Spelling* program results in significant gains in reading and spelling, including contextual fluency.

Then came the question of whether or not imagery could be directly and explicitly developed and applied to math skills. Could the theoretical model of dual coding be applied to competence in mathematical computation? Again, years of clinical and classroom research provided an answer. Yes, the conscious development and application of imagery for mathematical concepts and computation with the *On Cloud Nine Math* program results in significant gains in math skills.

As the effectiveness of the above programs validated the premise that weakness in imagery can be directly and explicitly stimulated and applied to different aspects of learning, the next question was whether dual coding could be stimulated and developed for children with severely delayed language development or for those with an autistic spectrum disorder. It seemed clear that these children might be the most impaired in terms of creating and accessing imagery, the important "other half" of the code. Could they be taught to consciously perceive the sensory information of imagery? Was their language and the sensory input of their imagery too weak to respond to instruction? Given that some children on the autistic spectrum had responded to *V/V*, what steps could we add that would standardize and simplify *V/V* for children with severe weakness in oral vocabulary and language expression?

To meet this need, we whittled *V/V* down to a lower level. What emerged is *Talkies*, a program with lots of little steps within big steps to develop the imagery-language connection. *V/V* gave birth to *Talkies*.

Talkies

The Process

The Steps of *Talkies*

1. **Climate**
2. **Sensory-Language Play**
   - Directed Play – (ST) plays; verb. what you see/pic as they play
   - Object Imagery – gest. size/shape w/ + w/o toy
   - Receptive Play with Nonverbal and Verbal Responses – thumbs ↑↓, then "up/down," "yes/no" (T) does 1st (ST) matches
   - Expressive Play with Verbal Responses – ① (T) talks + (ST) does – (T) does 1st – then (ST) does too ② (T) says ⇒ does ⇒ (ST) says ⇒ does ③ (ST) pic ⇒ says ⇒ does

   tell (ST) to pic what you will do, then match/act
3. **Talking Words**
   - Picture Structure Words – intro 2-3 + practice
   - Picture Vocabulary Cards – ① (T) says + (ST) points in group ② (T) points + (ST) says ③ img: show 2 sec, hide + QS
   - Vocabulary within Categories ① intro pg + have (ST) point to each ⇒ point out sim. ② (T) point + (ST) says ③ show pg 3 sec, hide, ⇒ recall ⇒ point out sim. ⇒ take a step game
   - Magic Window – isolate thing ('stop') + practice 3 str wds ⇒ ① (ST) names + ↓s cards
   - Magic Glass – ① use to isolate attributes ⇒ name ② show ⇒ hide
   - Magic Bag – (T) touches + describes ⇒ (ST) IDs ② (ST) peeks, imgs ⇒ describes
4. **Talking Sentences** ✗ Heart of program
   - Talking Two-Word Sentences * Give (ST) chk/(✓) often. Always flip over. mvmt. Prompt pic + do. * Say throughout + point. ⇒ img ~ no verb card ⇒ no animal
   - Talking Three-Word Sentences: Adjectives, Concepts, Articles, and Connectors – ① add color 1st ② concept ⇒ N end ③ once (T) + (ST) stable ⇒ add article (a/the)
   - Talking Four- to Seven-Word Sentences * pg 105-106 ⇒ building up sent.
   - Talking Sentences for Prosody – Voice inflection ⇒ connect to most imp. thing
5. **Simple Picture to Picture**
   - Object to Picture – Magic: place 2 toys behind door ⇒ (ST) picks + hides other ⇒ ✓ str wds ⇒ teacher guesses ⇒ open door if right
   - Shared Description of a Picture – place what, size, color, shape, numb. Direct pointing + (ST) verb. pic. ⇒ ✓ str wds ⇒ (T) summ. ⇒ (ST) summ.
   - Imagery Practice ⇒ same pic ⇒ hide ⇒ (ST) say + (T) Q to parts
   - * Picture to Picture – Magic door – simple pics ⇒ use "Your words make me..." "what should I pic..." ⇒ str. words ⇒ (T) summ. ⇒ ✓ pic is hidden from (T)

   * draw climate; Add "where"
6. **Simple Word Imaging**
   - Word to Object to Imagery
   - Word to Picture to Imagery
   - Known Noun Imaging
7. **Simple Sentence Imaging**
   - Visualizing and Verbalizing a Simple Sentence
8. **Talking Picture Stories**
   - Teacher Models a Picture Story
   - Visualizing and Verbalizing Picture Stories
9. **Simple Sentence by Sentence**

4 Chip and a Guide

This chapter is a guide for some of the critical pieces of this manual—parts to help you visualize and understand the whole of *Talkies*.

Chip

You met Chip in Chapter One and you will follow him through each step of *Talkies* to help you visualize the lessons. Picture Chip as a slightly chubby six year old with brown eyes and curly brown hair. He has difficulty expressing himself and comprehending language concepts, including following directions.

Chip has had speech therapy since he was three years old, a full-time tutor working with him on basic concepts since he was five years old, and ongoing consultations with medical professionals. Now in first grade, his poor communication skills are causing him social difficulty. He recognizes basic colors, has language for familiar toys and animals (like cow, car, truck, etc.), has generally good behavior (though he frustrates easily), and he has some sustained attention (though he needs a lot of reassurance).

Miss Billie

Having met Chip again, it is now time to meet Miss Billie. Miss Billie (for brevity, referred to as Billie in the sample lessons) is Chip's *Talkies* instructor, taking you through each step. Visualize her as a redheaded, passionate teacher, whose energy and skill is a model for the energy and skill needed to progress through the steps of *Talkies*. Miss Billie responds to Chip's responses and uses language to direct his attention to the sensory input of his imagery. Her energy keeps the joy in each session and she changes the activity or tasks when needed by letting him sit or lie on the floor to engage with her, or having him stand and take steps as a physical game while he completes tasks. She rarely expects him to just sit and listen, and when she does, it is for short periods of time. She motivates him by immediately rewarding his positive responses to help him focus and attend, and enjoy his time with her. Some of her students are more difficult than Chip, and some are easier in terms of both their behavior and their ability to communicate. In any case, she knows the importance of consistency in her language and interaction with Chip. Chip can count on what Miss Billie will say, how she will say it, and what she will do. He learns to trust her.

Language to Drive the Sensory Bus

As part of *V/V* or *Talkies* instruction, developmental or remedial, use instructional language that directly stimulates the sensory input of imagery. Remember Pribram's statement, "We cannot think about something of which we are not consciously aware, and we cannot be aware of something not perceived sufficiently at the sensory level to come to consciousness." Drive the sensory bus with your language to bring imagery to consciousness for your student—ask his sensory system to create mental representations for language.

The language of "What are you *picturing*..." directly stimulates imagery, whereas, the language of "What are you *thinking*..." does not. The language of "What do you picture will happen next..." is better than "What do you think will happen next...." In vocabulary development, note the difference in sensory stimulation for the following questions. "What do you *picture* for the word *skyscraper*?" "What is the *meaning* of the word *skyscraper*?"

The word *picture* in your language brings imagery to a conscious level as a sensory tool the child may begin to use spontaneously, improving his problem solving, comprehension, and critical thinking even when not in the instructional environment.

Socratic Learning: Question, Compare the Response to the Stimulus, Give Choices

Our *Talkies* students have to be led with questions to discover the sensory information in their sensory system. Therefore, it is imperative to create a Socratic learning environment, a give and take, a back and forth with your student. You ask questions to stimulate sensory processing and cognition. You ask for a response from your student. To stimulate more thinking and sensory experiences, you need to respond to your student's response. As he begins to trust that you will react positively to his every response, he will respond with more energy and more attention.

Questioning your student, rather than telling him, means you are likely to find errors in his responses. Those errors are to be viewed as positives, not negatives; an error is an opportunity for additional questioning to further stimulate sensory information. Errors that are handled in a supportive manner continue to develop sensory-cognitive processing and take advantage of precious instruction time. There are four basic principles for error handling: (1) note the student's response, (2) find a spot in his response from which to positively engage him, (3) help him analyze his response, and (4) help him compare his response to the stimulus.

Daily Instruction

Daily instruction is an important element for success in the development of sensory-cognitive processing, especially with children severely impaired in perceiving sensory input at a conscious level. Intensive instruction, two to four hours a day, is an even more important element for success with *Talkies* students. Repetitive stimulation is needed to develop strong pathways for the sensory processing to become automatic.

Behavior Motivation and Rewards

A *Talkies* student needs external motivation to keep his much needed engagement and attention to process sensory information. Throughout the little steps of *Talkies*, small, constant rewards are given immediately for positive behavior or responses, no matter how small the success. Using manipulatives (small objects) for a reward is a nonverbal way to acknowledge a response, a success, or a behavior. Because of the difficulty a *Talkies* student experiences receiving and expressing language, he may have acquired a habit of tuning out language. Since the language hasn't been processed, he may have begun to ignore it.

Rewards can get his attention while you stimulate and develop his ability to dual code by responding to his response as you drive the sensory bus. Using an object for the reward enables you to give the reward or take it away throughout the lesson, with no verbalization from you. For example, if the student is doing a behavior you want to control or change, you can quietly take away a stone, without verbal condemnation that the student may ignore anyhow. The student will usually notice when you take away a stone or something he has earned. Then you can give a brief explanation of why it was moved, and if the behavior improves put the stone back.

Tactile, colorful objects such as the Magic Stones in the *Talkies* Kit lend themselves to immediate behavior reinforcement and motivation. The Magic Stones are shiny, brightly colored plastic gems that look like pirate treasure and can be kept in the student's personal Magic Stone bag, a small treasure box, or a plastic jar that lets the student see the accumulated stones. While the stones are a favorite, you can substitute other objects as long as they can be brought in and out of the stimulation as a reward.

If a student loses interest in the Magic Stones, or whatever you are using for rewards, switch to something else such as peanuts, beans, or appropriate manipulatives that are large enough to not be choking hazards but are small enough to be kept in the student's bag or jar. The goal is to have an object that can be added or removed, as well as accumulated for a prize/reward. Sometimes, to renew interest in rewards, connect the reward to a student's specific interest. For example, Chip loved toy cars, so points (marks on a paper) were accumulated for him to earn a small toy car.

Consistency

Consistency in the teacher's language and behavior is important for *Talkies* students, especially in the early steps of the instruction. Not only should your vocabulary be as simple as possible, your language should also be consistent, especially with language that drives the sensory bus. The student needs to become familiar with your terms, your phrases, and your demeanor. Your energy should be consistently passionate and positive. The energy with which instruction is delivered, in *Talkies* or any program, is nearly as important as the steps of the program. Positive energy is something that can be seen and felt, like an electrifying connection that can't be cut.

Oral Vocabulary: Imagery and Speed

As everyone knows, oral vocabulary is a primary sensory-cognitive factor in receptive and expressive language processing—and usually a *Talkies* student has weak oral vocabulary. The stimulation of imagery for vocabulary development continues throughout *Talkies*, using a personal vocabulary chart, lists, or 3x5 cards to track words the student images easily (knows) and the words he needs to image faster and more vividly (doesn't know).

The speed of processing words is a critical factor in receptive and expressive language processing for both oral and written language. Written language contextual fluency requires words to be placed in memory for accurate, quick access. Sight words are established through symbol imagery, the mental representation of letters in words that is needed for memory. Without a well-established sight word base, students will read slowly or guess from context, both interfering with comprehension.

The same issue of speed and accuracy applies to oral language contextual fluency and comprehension. Students need to quickly and accurately access the meaning of words; the images of words in their oral language lexicon. And the speed of processing is more important for oral language than written language. Written language can be reread but oral language cannot. Oral language comes into the sensory system quickly, word after word, sentence after sentence. The words and sentences have to not only be processed accurately but they have to be processed rapidly. Students need to quickly and accurately access mental representations for words and bring those mental representations to a whole. Teach vocabulary for both speed and accuracy.

Practice and Pacing

Each chapter has a Practice and Pacing section, and while each step might be slightly different to practice and pace, there are basic concepts to note throughout the program: (1) lesson energy, (2) task levels, (3) overlapping of steps, and (4) self-correction and automaticity.

When stimulating and developing imagery, automaticity is a diagnostic marker. It took many years of working with students to learn that speed in creating and accessing imagery is critical for self-correcting, self-generating, independent language processing. Language comes at our sensory system very quickly. As noted above, when the creation and acquisition of imagery is slow, language may tumble by before it can be imaged and processed. Remember, imagery is half of the cognitive code. Note behaviors such as eyes looking up or defocusing (which are signs of imaging), but also note the speed in which that imagery is being accessed. A student may show evidence of beginning to create mental representations, but if he has to slow down or stop to create images, the world of communication may pass him by. He may remain stuck on a part rather than imaging the whole.

Charts to See Tasks and Progress

Talkies students need to know what they are doing and how well they are doing it. Since they don't process language well, their tasks and progress need to be communicated to them in a visual form—a task chart with task cards.

Put tasks on a flannel board or a pocket chart, and be sure the tasks are designated with a picture and/or written label. If your student can't decode yet, he needs a pictorial representation of the task. To make a task card, put the name of the task on the card and then illustrate it. To keep the student active and involved in the lesson, have him turn the card over when the task is complete. If you put the task cards on a flannel board, use a large arrow that he can move from task to task.

The importance of a task chart cannot be overstated. A student with limited receptive and expressive language often lives in a world of jumbled, unrelated words and concepts. The task chart helps him understand what is expected in each lesson, often reducing his anxiety and increasing his attention.

Keep Sessions Active

The student needs to attend to sensory input that you will activate with your questions. Yet he is unlikely to bring a significant amount of attention to the learning environment. Therefore, along with immediate rewards and consistency in your language, change the tasks and the learning environment to help sustain his attention. Observe his behavior and as soon as you note his attention waning, change what he is doing or where he is doing it. If he has been sitting at a table, put him on the floor. If he is on the floor, have him stand and take a step when he responds as you want, sometimes have him step backward to where he started. Do physical activities in between tasks such as having him jump or hop three times and then sit down to start the next task.

Create a game with the task you are working on. A simple game to put a vocabulary card to "sleep" is a way to change an activity and keep attention. For example, as your student names a vocabulary card, turn the card over to put it to "sleep." Or put the vocabulary cards in a make-believe basket when they are named. Or create a "race" by letting your student keep a card he can name as it races toward him.

Gesturing

Gesturing represents imagery and enhances verbal descriptions. A good storyteller links imagery with language through gestures. Many children with weak expressive language also do not use gestures when they talk, probably as good an indication as any that they are also not imaging vividly. Encourage gesturing throughout *Talkies*. Your student can feel a ball and then gesture or show you what he felt. He can act out familiar movements such as running, jumping, and hopping.

Sample Lessons

Each step has a Sample Lesson that presents the teacher-student interaction and each lesson has two parts: the interactive Lesson and the Lesson Summary, a short, itemized summary.

Summary Pages for Each Step

A Summary at the end of each chapter concisely summarizes the salient points of each *Talkies* step. First a part of the *V/V* manual, and later a part of *On Cloud Nine* and *Seeing Stars*, the Summary pages have received rave reviews as an aid to the instruction. Also included in the Appendix, the Summary pages enable you to view the whole of *Talkies* at a glance to more easily implement the entire program.

Small Group and Classroom Instruction

Each Summary gives suggestions for group instruction, however, the basic steps of *Talkies* do not have to be modified for group instruction, no matter the size of the group. In effect, you will look at the group as one big sensory system, while at the same time keeping your big eyes and big ears on each individual child.

Let's Fly

The Story of the Geese was presented in *Seeing Stars* as a metaphor for teaching. Geese fly in a V formation to uplift all the geese in the flock. When a goose gets sick or wounded, two geese drop out of the formation, one on each side, and take him down to the ground to protect him. They stay with the goose, never leaving him, until he grows well again.

When Chip came to us, he was out of formation, unable to fly with the flock. In the next chapters of *Talkies*, we will make him well. We will teach him to process language and reach his potential.

Remember, you can do this. You can do anything.

Let's fly.

The Climate: A Short What and Why

It is important for students to know what they are going to do with you and why, but keep your explanation short, especially for a *Talkies* student. If your explanation is too long, it may become gibberish to Chip. Simplify the explanation as much as possible: draw and talk.

SAMPLE LESSON

Setting the Climate

Billie: "I want you to make pictures in your mind. Like for the word *tree*." She draws a head with a tree in a thought bubble as she talks.

Billie: "We can say *tree*. We can picture a tree."

Chip doesn't talk during the climate, and Miss Billie doesn't ask him to talk. Her goal is to briefly explain what and why, and move on to the next step.

If it seems your student does not understand the climate presentation, don't make the mistake of thinking that a longer, more detailed explanation will help him understand. On the contrary, more verbalization from you is likely to result in a negative, rather than a positive. Lost in a swirl of words, your student may become distracted and lose interest in working with you. You will have lost not only his attention, but also precious learning time when you could have been stimulating imagery. Therefore, rather than talking more, start the dual coding stimulation, and briefly re-set the climate throughout the little steps of *Talkies* instruction.

Summary: Step 1

Climate

Goal: To briefly explain to the student *what* and *why*.

1. Setting the Climate

- Make a head with a thought bubble, then draw the tree as you explain:
- "We will picture words in your mind."
- "We can say *tree*."
- "We can picture a tree."

6 Sensory-Language Play

The goal of Sensory-Language Play is to engage the student, establish reciprocity, and begin an awareness of the imagery-language connection. During this step, note the reciprocity between you and the student. Is he engaged with you, making eye contact, responding to you as you respond to him? Is he closing the circle of communication? Watch for moments of connection. Sometimes the engagement may be slight, such as a gesture, and sometimes it may be eye contact, with or without verbal expression. In general, reciprocity may be matching your movement, eye contact, facial expression, body language, gestures, emotions, and verbal communication. Look and listen as the diagnostician.

Along with establishing a connection with the student, Sensory-Language Play introduces the concept of imagery to language. Introduce the language of "picturing" to the instruction to start the process of bringing that sensory input to consciousness. Think of these first two steps of *Talkies* as an introduction to imagery rather than the establishment of imagery. Since your student may not understand what you mean by "picturing" or "imagery," simply begin to expose him to the vocabulary and demonstrate the connection between imagery and language when you play and model tasks.

Let's begin the little steps in Sensory-Language Play by starting at the beginning of language acquisition—play.

Play to Establish Rapport

Play is an important first step in establishing a connection with a child. The first little step in Sensory-Language Play is to follow the student's lead and play with the toys

to establish trust, engagement, and reciprocity. As you are playing, also direct the play to the imagery-language connection by referring to picturing as part of your thinking process and as part of the communication between yourself and the student.

In the first session with Chip, Miss Billie starts the connection with, "Let's play with these toys!" Getting a bag of toys, she lets Chip choose toys and begin to play with them. As he plays, Miss Billie engages with him, verbalizing what he is doing, talking about her own imagery, and noting his response to her. As she responds to his responses, she closes the circle of communication between herself and Chip. If the student is engaging in Floortime activities, this will be a comfortable beginning environment for him.

Object Imagery

As the student begins to engage with you, overlap to the second little step in Sensory-Language Play. Play by having the student visualize an object that is given and then taken away (hidden). It is important to introduce the concept of imagery with an object to picture. By giving the student an object to see and touch, the visual and kinesthetic input will assist him with imagery-recall.

Beginning where Chip left off in the first little step, Miss Billie presents the concept of imagery, giving him an object to visualize.

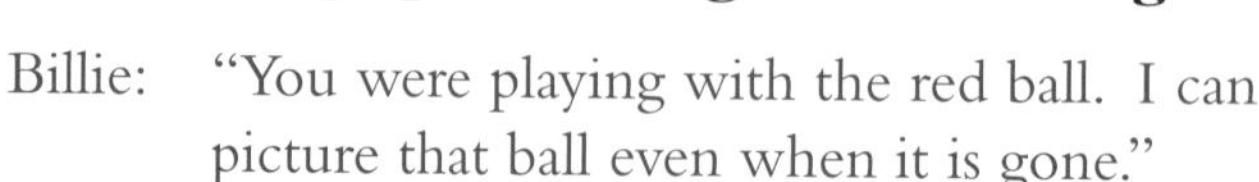

Object Imagery: Touching and Gesturing

Billie: "You were playing with the red ball. I can picture that ball even when it is gone."

Chip: He watches.

Billie: "When I picture something, I see it in my mind. Here is a red ball." She touches the red ball. "Now when I take it away, I can still picture the red ball in my mind. It is like this." She gestures the shape/size of the ball.

Chip: He watches.

Billie: Quickly re-setting the climate, she draws a head and a thought bubble with a ball in it. "See, I can picture the ball in my mind."

Chip: He watches.

Billie: "Now it is your turn. Feel the ball all over. Close your eyes. Now open them and look at the ball again."

Chip: He touches the ball, closes his eyes quickly, and then opens them.

Billie: "Now, the ball is gone. Show me with your hands what you pictured for the ball."

Chip: Silent, he quickly gestures something in front of him. Miss Billie takes his hands and helps him make the shape of the ball.

Billie: "Great. You showed me what you pictured. Let's do another one."

Lesson Summary:

Object Imagery: Touching and Gesturing

- Student is given a simple, known object.
- Student feels the object with his eyes open and then closed.
- With the object taken away, the student gestures the object's size and shape.
- Teacher may help the student gesture.

With object imagery introduced, Chip and Miss Billie do a few more and then move to the next little step, receptive play. She continues to do object imaging while she overlaps to the next steps. She knows Chip's imagery is still not strong, vivid, or brought to consciousness.

Receptive Play: Student Judges Right or Wrong with Nonverbal Response

In Receptive Play, the student is the "teacher" and judges your responses. Once he can judge whether you are wrong or right, then he can judge whether he is wrong or right. [Monitoring his responses is a prerequisite to self-correction and independence.]

In the lesson below, Chip learns the nonverbal thumbs-up or thumbs-down gesture so he can participate in the receptive practice. If the concept of thumbs-up or thumbs-down is too difficult for your student, or if you just want a change, make some thumbs-up and thumbs-down cards or use the cards in the *Talkies* Kit. It is sometimes fun to replace the gesture with a card, especially when working with groups of students.

SAMPLE LESSON

Receptive Play with Thumbs-Up or Thumbs-Down Nonverbal Response

Billie: "Let me show you that head I drew." Miss Billie re-sets the climate with the head and the thought bubble to reintroduce imagery to Chip. "Give me a thumbs-up, like this, if this is a head." Miss Billie demonstrates thumbs-up, takes his hand, and helps him do the thumbs-up gesture.

Chip: He does a thumbs-up.

Billie: "Great! Thumbs-up means I did it right! Here's a Magic Stone for you because you did thumbs-up."

Billie: "Here is your head. Here you are picturing the tree." She quickly draws a sketch of a tree in the thought bubble as she talks. "Did I draw a tree or an elephant? If it was a tree, give me thumbs-up. If not, give me thumbs-down."

Chip: Watching her draw, Chip gives her a thumbs-up.

Billie: "Great! You're right. I drew a tree. Get yourself a stone!"

Chip: Smiling, he gets himself a stone.

Billie: "If you want to get another stone, use your words and say *thumbs-up*!"

Chip: He smiles. "Up." He does the thumbs-up gesture.

Billie: "Great. Get yourself another stone. Let's keep going. I'm going to picture something in my mind." She squints her eyes to show that she is picturing. "I picture a red truck. You touch the red truck."

Chip: Silent, he touches the red truck.

Billie: "Great. I'll give you thumbs-up and a Magic Stone. Now let's do more."

Billie: "I'm sticking out my tongue. Thumbs-up or down?" She blinks her eyes but doesn't stick out her tongue.

Chip: Smiling, he gives a thumbs-down.

Extending the offer to the student to verbalize is a good overlap, but verbalizing should not be demanded. The focus of this little step is for your student to judge wrong or right with a nonverbal response.

Lesson Summary:
Receptive Play with Thumbs-Up or Thumbs-Down Nonverbal Response

- Student learns nonverbal thumbs-up or thumbs-down gesture, or uses thumbs-up or thumbs-down cards.
- Using a toy, the teacher visualizes, verbalizes, and does an action.
- Student judges right or wrong with thumbs-up or thumbs-down gesture, or card.

Receptive Play: Student Judges with Verbal Response

The receptive practice continues but now with a verbal response. The student continues to monitor responses before being asked to perform a task.

With Chip learning how to monitor an action with the nonverbal thumbs-up and thumbs-down gesture, the next little step asks him to add a verbal response to the nonverbal gesture. Miss Billie believes Chip can verbalize right or wrong and she gives him that choice. However, she limits the choices for some of her more difficult students.

SAMPLE LESSON

Receptive Play with Verbal Response

Billie: "Now you are the teacher again. This time you get to tell me if I'm right or wrong. You get to say *up* or *down*, or *right* or *wrong*."

Billie: "I'm picturing the red car on my nose." She takes the red car, holds it on her nose. "Give me a thumbs-up and say *up* if I put the red car on my nose."

Chip: "Up." He does the thumbs-up gesture.

Billie: "Great! Get two stones! Let's play more. I'm picturing the red car on my foot. Picture that, too. Now, I'm putting the red car on my foot." She talks as she does the action, something that is becoming a constant for Chip.

Billie: "Tell me *right* if I did what I pictured and said."

Chip: "Right." He gives the nonverbal thumbs-up.

Billie: "Good job. You can say *up* or you can say *right*. I'll give you a Magic Stone every time you talk to me about what I did. I picture a blue ball on my hand. Picture

that!" She waits just a second to give him time to visualize, and then puts the blue ball on her hand. "Thumbs-up or down, right or wrong?"

Chip: "Right." He holds his thumb up.

Billie: "Great. I was right. How about this? I picture the blue ball on my head. Picture that." She waits a second and puts the blue ball on her foot. "Did I put the blue ball on my head?"

Chip: "No." He gives the thumbs-down gesture.

Billie: "Good job. I didn't put it on my head!"

> **Lesson Summary:**
> ***Receptive Play with Verbal Response***
>
> - Using a toy, teacher visualizes, verbalizes, and does an action.
> - Student can verbalize *right, wrong, up, down, yes,* or *no*.
> - Student may also use nonverbal thumbs up or thumbs-down gesture.

The interaction with your student may not go as well as this, or it may go better. In any case, remember to work the little steps forward and backward, doing a step only as long as you need to and overlapping from step to step to change the activity.

Expressive Play with Action, Nonverbal, and Verbal Responses

This little step of Expressive Play has even smaller steps within it. With imagery discussed in each littler step, first the teacher talks and the student does. Second, the teacher does and the student talks. Third, the student does it all, he talks and does.

In the first smaller step below, Miss Billie visualizes, verbalizes, and does. Chip matches her action and verbalizes *right* or *wrong*.

SAMPLE LESSON

Expressive Play #1: Teacher Talks and Student Does

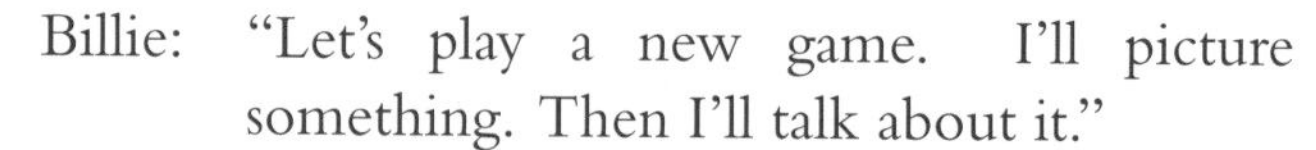

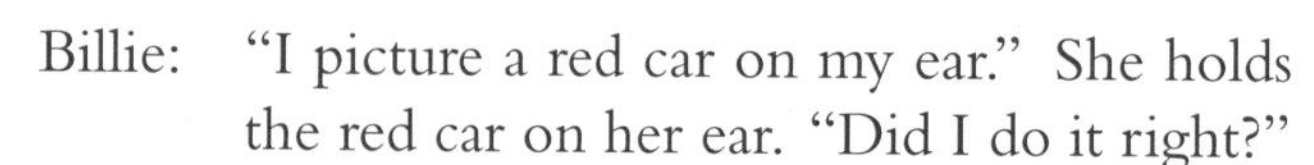

Billie: "Let's play a new game. I'll picture something. Then I'll talk about it."

Billie: "I picture a red car on my ear." She holds the red car on her ear. "Did I do it right?"

Chip: "Right." He does a thumbs-up.

Billie: "Good. Now it is your turn. Picture that red car on your ear, and then do it."

Chip: He takes the red car and holds it on his ear.

Billie: "Right!" She gestures thumbs-up. "You put a red car on your ear. Get yourself a Magic Stone. Let's do some more. I picture the blue airplane flying up." She picks up the airplane and pretends it is flying up, making a whirring sound. "You picture it and then make the airplane fly."

Chip: He picks up the airplane, moves it into the air, making a whirring sound.

Billie: "Great job! You matched me. Get some stones!"

Lesson Summary:
Expressive Play #1: Teacher Talks and Student Does

- Using a toy, the teacher visualizes, verbalizes, and does.
- Student judges right or wrong, verbally and nonverbally.
- Student pictures the action and does it too.

Practice the above until fairly stable, making sure to give immediate rewards. Continue to use the nonverbal thumbs-up or thumbs-down gesture with the verbal wrong/right (or yes/no) and then overlap to the next little step where the teacher talks and the student verbalizes what she did, matching his verbalization with an action.

SAMPLE LESSON

Expressive Play #2: Teacher Does and Student Talks

Billie: "I'm picturing putting the blue airplane in my hand. You win when you can tell me what I did!" She puts the airplane in her hand. "Tell me what I did."

Chip: "Airplane hand."

Billie: "Great. I put the airplane in my hand. You can get two stones if you tell me what I did again. This time tell me the color of the airplane."

Chip: "Blue airplane hand."

Billie: "Great. Let's make it more fun. I'll picture it. I'll do it. You talk to me and then you do it, too."

Billie: "I'm picturing the red ball on my head." She holds the ball on her head. "Tell me what I did and then you can do it."

Chip: "Red ball head." He puts the red ball on his head.

Billie: "Great. You told me the color of the ball, too. Get three stones this time!"

Lesson Summary:
Expressive Play #2: Teacher Does and Student Talks

- Using a toy, the teacher visualizes, verbalizes, and does an action.
- Student verbalizes the action.
- Student does the action.

The lessons continue until there is some consistency in the student's response. The lessons should not continue so long as to lose the joy and energy of the instruction. Instead, overlap back to an easier task and then overlap forward to a little harder task.

Your lessons may require more or less practice and interaction than what you are observing with Chip. In any case, work the little steps of *Talkies* as though the steps are holding hands with each other. Sometimes only one or two steps hold hands, and sometimes three or four steps hold hands. Overlapping the steps allows you to change the tasks, keep attention and lesson energy, and still move toward the goal of developing his ability to dual code imagery and language. There is no such thing as going "back," the steps are being worked together—just little steps holding hands to teach Chip to fly.

In the next little step of Expressive Play, the student pictures, talks, and does. Let's look in on Chip doing it all.

SAMPLE LESSON

Expressive Play #3:
Student Talks and Does

Billie: "It is your turn to be the teacher! Picture one of the toys doing something. Then say it and do it!"

Chip: "Tiger runs." He picks up the tiger and runs around the room with it.

Billie: "Great. Picture doing something else. Say it. Then do it."

Chip: "Tiger jumps." He holds the tiger in his hand and jumps up and down.

You do not know if your student is visualizing or not, though you can look for signs of imagery such as his eyes going up or defocusing. Even if you do see a sign of imagery, you don't have a window into his head to know the vividness or speed of his imagery. So you keep going. You continue to use the word "picturing" as part of your shared vocabulary, never knowing when the light may go on in his sensory system. You continue to make every session include references to imagery in an effort to bring his own imagery to a conscious level.

Lesson Summary:
Expressive Play #3: Student Talks and Does

- Student pictures, talks, and does.
- Student takes a toy and says what action he will make the toy do.
- Student does the action with the toy.

Error Handling

You must question the student to bring sensory input to a conscious level that can be perceived, stored, and accessed. However, a questioning interaction with the student means the student must respond in some way, verbally or nonverbally. Some of those responses may be incorrect.

An incorrect response is a positive, not a negative, because the response can be used to help the student compare his response to the stimulus. He learns that his responses are directly connected to a stimulus and that they close a circle of interaction. Start your interaction at the student's response; meet him where he is and help him analyze his answer to your question. Always start with a positive. Here is an example of error handling. Watch how Miss Billie meets Chip at his response.

SAMPLE LESSON

Error Handling for Expressive Play #3: Student Talks and Does

ERROR: Chip demonstrates the wrong movement for the sentence.

Billie: "It is your turn to be the teacher! Picture one of the toys doing something, then say and do it!"

Chip: "Tiger runs." He picks up the tiger and makes it jump up and down in one spot.

Billie: "Good. You made the tiger move. You showed me the tiger moving like this." She shows the tiger jumping. "This is *jump*. You said, 'Tiger runs.' Show me *run*. You run."

Chip: Chip gets up and runs.

Billie: "Great. That is running. Show me the tiger running."

Chip: Chip makes the tiger run.

Billie: "Great. Now show me *Tiger jumps*."

Note that Miss Billie didn't stop when Chip made the correct response and showed her the tiger running. Instead, she used his error to contrast the difference between run and jump.

There are many ways Miss Billie might have handled the interaction. She might have simply had him recognize that he made the tiger jump and then he would have self-corrected. Or she might have had him recognize that he made the tiger jump and then shown him the movement *run*, contrasting *jump* to *run*. In the above, she chose to have him show her the movement *run*; she might also have had him show her *jump*, so he would experience the contrast between *jump* and *run*.

No matter which direction you take in error handling, start with these basic principles: (1) note the student's response, (2) find a spot in the student's response from which to positively engage him, (3) help the student analyze his response, and

(4) help the student compare his response to the stimulus. You can often go one step further and contrast his response to the accurate response; however, you don't want to question him so long as to lose his attention

Practice and Pacing

The directed play with toys may continue as a preface to each little step if it is needed, but not longer. Overlap the little steps in *Talkies*, thinking of each step as a part of a whole. When a step is strong enough to drop, extend the process by holding hands with a higher step, traveling up the ladder of steps toward the whole. At this point you may be doing the first few steps of Sensory-Language Play and focusing on object imagery and receptive/expressive play as you extend into the first part of Talking Words.

Along with practicing the little steps of *Talkies*, you *may* be able to add a "game" to call conscious attention to the length of eye contact. Use a stopwatch to time yourself and the student during a simple staring contest—the "Eye Game." First see who can sustain eye contact longer between you and your student, and then have your student try to beat his own time. You can play the game three or more times at a setting during instruction, as a break, or just for fun.

Summary: Step 2

Sensory-Language Play

Goal: Engage the student, establish reciprocity, and begin an awareness of the imagery-language connection. Following the student's lead, imagery and language are introduced and extended into receptive and expressive play with nonverbal and verbal responses.

1. Play to Establish Rapport

- Student is encouraged to "play" with toys.
- Student begins to be comfortable with the environment.
- Student begins to be comfortable with teacher.
- Teacher notes reciprocity and affective processing.

2. Object Imagery: Touching and Gesturing

- Student is given a simple, known object.
- Student feels the object with his eyes open and then closed.
- With the object taken away, the student gestures the object's size and shape.
- Teacher may help the student gesture.

3. Receptive Play with Thumbs-Up or Thumbs-Down Nonverbal Response

- Student learns nonverbal thumbs-up or thumbs-down gesture, or uses thumbs-up or thumbs-down cards.
- Using a toy, the teacher visualizes, verbalizes, and does an action.
- Student judges right or wrong with thumbs-up or thumbs-down gesture, or card.

4. Receptive Play with Verbal Response

- Using a toy, teacher visualizes, verbalizes, and does an action.
- Student can verbalize *right, wrong, up, down, yes,* or *no*.
- Student may also use nonverbal thumbs up or thumbs-down gesture.

5. Expressive Play with Action, Nonverbal, and Verbal Responses

a. Expressive Play #1: Teacher Talks and Student Does
   - Using a toy, the teacher visualizes, verbalizes, and does.
   - Student judges right or wrong, verbally and nonverbally.
   - Student pictures the action and does it too.

b. Expressive Play #2: Teacher Does and Student Talks
   - Using a toy, the teacher visualizes, verbalizes, and does an action.
   - Student verbalizes the action.
   - Student does the action.

c. Expressive Play #3: Student Talks and Does
   - Student pictures, talks, and does.
   - Student takes a toy and says what action he will make the toy do.
   - Student does the action with the toy.

Group Instruction

The process of the Sensory-Language Play step requires no modification for small group or classroom instruction, but as in all group instruction, group management techniques need to be employed.

- When first playing to build rapport, encourage all the students to play with the toys and then engage with each individual in turn.
- In Object Imagery, have the students take turns with the object, feeling it, imaging it, and gesturing to their image.
- In Receptive Play with Nonverbal Response, have all the students respond with a thumbs-up or thumbs-down gesture, and then question various students to ensure his or her responses are appropriate.
- In the Receptive and Expressive Play with Verbal Response, all students can respond nonverbally with a thumbs-up or thumbs-down while they take turns giving verbal responses.

Suggested Books and Products

The following books and products are suggested for vocabulary and concept development:

First Concepts Numbers by Robert Tarnish

First Concepts Opposites by Melanie Whittington

Language Builder Picture Cards by Stages® Learning Materials

Learning Block Books, 26 Board Books in a Box! illustrated by Susan Estelle Kwas and designed by Paul Kepple

My Big Animal Book by Roger Priddy

My Little Word Book by Roger Priddy

Scholastic First Picture Dictionary by Geneviève de la Bretesche and illustrated by Charlotte Voake

Slide 'N' Seek Opposites by Chuck Murphy

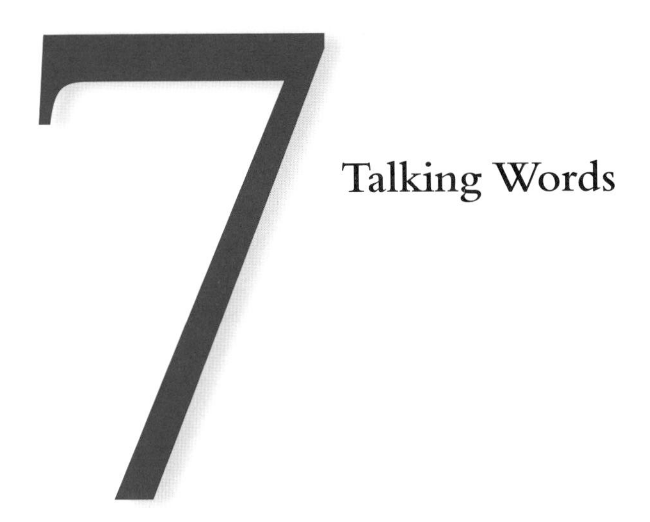

Talking Words

The goal of Talking Words is to develop imagery for oral vocabulary and basic concepts. As dual coding is developing, new vocabulary is organized and categorized to increase the student's word retrieval for expressive language. As Healy (2004) states, "Children who can 'see' relationships and organize input at a sensory level seem to have an easier time organizing thoughts and ideas."

The big step of Talking Words has lots of little steps, ranging from picture cards through the Magic Bag. The sequence of the stimulation is receptive, expressive, and imagery practice. Each little step ends with direct stimulation of imagery.

A Look at Chip Now

As we look in on Miss Billie and Chip, he is midway into his third week of *Talkies*. He is beginning to trust Miss Billie, making eye contact more often and smiling more frequently. He is starting to respond. Miss Billie watches and listens closely as they interact, but there is no outward signs of imagery, such as his eyes going up or defocusing. However, she holds the big picture in her mind and continues to drive the sensory bus to bring imagery to consciousness for Chip.

Picture Structure Words as Conceptual Pegs

The *V/V* structure words represent the important elements to be visualized with language—the conceptual pegs. For *Talkies*, however, two important adjustments are made to the *V/V* procedures to reduce the task to the smallest steps possible: (1) the structure words are illustrated, and (2) only a few structure words are introduced.

The number of structure words introduced in *Talkies* is reduced to *what*, *movement*, *color*, *size*, *shape*, *number*, and *where*. Illustrate your own structure words or use the simply illustrated Picture Structure Word Cards in the *Talkies* Kit. The Picture Structure Word *movement* has action figures, *what* has a variety of toys/figures to represent nouns, *size* has a range of sizes, and *color* has a pallet of primary colors.

Let's spend some time with them as Miss Billie introduces the *what* and *movement* structure words. Chip has completed a few tasks of receptive and expressive play, has a pile of Magic Stones, and just got through running around the room with a cow.

SAMPLE LESSON

Introduction of Picture Structure Words

Movement Picture Structure Word

Billie: "We've had fun with those toys. Now let's play with these special cards." She puts the *movement*, *what*, and *color* structure word cards on the floor where she and Chip are now sitting.

Billie: "See? The cards have words and pictures. Touch each of them."

Chip: He touches each card.

Billie: "Good job. Get a stone."

Chip: He picks through the stones for the big red stone and drops it in his treasure chest.

Billie: "Now touch the card with the colors on it."

Chip: He touches the *color* structure word card.

Billie: "Right! Thumbs-up. Turn the card over and put it to sleep. Now we have two cards. Which one shows things moving?"

Chip: He turns over the *color* card and touches the *movement* card.

Billie: "Good job! That shows things moving, like running and jumping. Let's do some moving. Let's hop." She takes Chip's hand and they hop a little bit.

Billie: "Whew." She sits down again. "We hopped. If you say *hop*, you can hop again!"

Chip: "Hop." Smiling, Chip gets up and hops around.

Billie: "Oh, so great! Get two stones, one for hopping and one for saying, 'hop.'"

Chip: He gets two stones, smiling. "Hop."

Billie: "Great! Now, let's do another movement. Let's run."

What Picture Structure Word

Miss Billie does a few more actions with the *movement* structure word, and then introduces *what*.

Billie: "You did some movements for this card. Put the card to sleep. Turn it over."

Chip: He turns over the *movement* card.

Billie: "Good job." She touches the *what* card. "Touch this card with me. Let's show this card with some toys from our basket. Pick a toy."

Chip: He chooses a little red truck.

Billie: "Great. Tell me what that is." She probes for the language processing and the connection she has made with him in previous lessons, noting reciprocity. She wants to know if he can name the truck, but if he can't, she'll give him choices.

Chip: "Truck. Red truck."

Billie: "Right! Thumbs-up. This is a red truck. Get three extra stones for telling me what color it is!"

Chip: Smiling, he carefully picks out three special stones.

Billie: "Let's see if you can find some more *whats*. I'm going to put some toys on the table. Find the toy I say." She puts a train, a pig, and a tiger on the table. "Find the train."

Chip: He points to the train on the table.

Billie: "Great. That is a train. If you say *train*, you can get a stone."

Chip: "Train."

Billie: "Great. Let's keep playing. Find another what. Pick up the pig."

Chip: He picks up the pig.

Billie: "Right. Here is a stone. You can get another stone if you put that back and tell me what it is."

Chip: "Pig." He puts the pig back on the table, and starts to pick up the red car.

Billie: "Right. That was a pig. What are you picking up?"

Chip: "Car."

Billie: "Right! Say *car* and tell me the color of the car."

Chip: "Red car."

Billie: "Right! Let's get on the floor and play a game with all the toys." She dumps the bag of toys on the floor. "Find the blue airplane." She uses the adjective *blue*, because there is also a red plastic airplane and a green

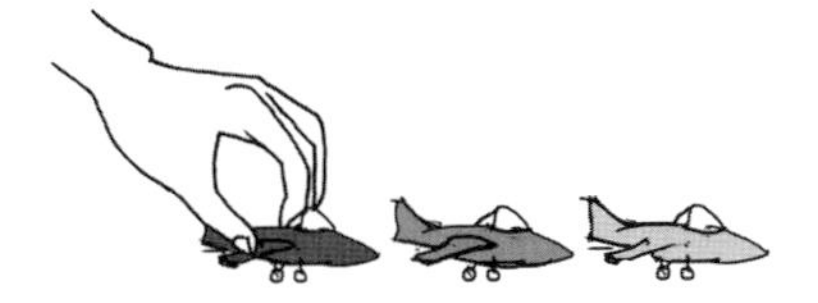

plastic airplane and she wants him to start to choose from smaller contrasts.

Chip: He correctly gets the blue airplane.

Billie: "Great. If you say *airplane*, you can get more stones."

Chip: "Airplane. Blue airplane."

Miss Billie continues to work on different "whats" and checks to see if Chip can also say and find a *what* by himself. For example, she has him find things around the room, such as a chair, a picture, a table, and a door.

Color Picture Structure Word

Billie: "Let's wake up this card." She turns over the *color* structure word card. "See, this card has different colors on it. We are going to play a game about colors. I'm going to put two toys on the table and I want you to find the one that is red."

Chip: He points to the red toy truck.

Billie: "Right. Thumbs-up. The truck is red. Tell me what it is."

Chip: "Red truck."

Billie: "Good job. Here are two stones. Let's walk around the room and see how many red things you can find. I'll put a piece of popcorn in my cup for you every time you touch something red. And, I'll give you another piece of popcorn if you tell me the name of what you touch." (She had gotten permission from his mother to give him popcorn.) They walk around the room touching objects that are red. Chip says, "red," and sometimes he says the name of the thing he touches.

Lesson Summary:
Introduction of Picture Structure Words

- Teacher names a structure word.
- Student finds and touches the appropriate card.
- Teacher concretizes the structure word with toys, movements, and contrast.

Picturing Vocabulary! Cards to Stimulate Single-Word Imagery for Oral Vocabulary

The *Talkies* Kit includes the *Picturing Vocabulary!* Cards to stimulate single-word imagery and establish familiar and new oral vocabulary. While you may choose to use other vocabulary picture cards, it is important to use a card that illustrates a word without extraneous pictorial information.

There are a high volume of picture vocabulary cards available on the market, but many have too much pictorial information on the card, often camouflaging the illustrated word. For example, one card has a picture of a woman walking up steps, outside, with a brick wall on her left and plants growing on the top of the wall. You see her from the back, clothed in a sweater and pants, as she walks up the steps toward an apartment house, with a car in front of a garage, animals in view, and potted plants in the yard and on the window sills. The picture card is for the word *up*, but the concept of *up* cannot easily be visually discerned from the other pictorial information in the picture.

Picturing Vocabulary! Cards for Single-Word Imagery

Picturing Vocabulary! Cards are first practiced receptively and expressively, and then imagery practice is added to store words in memory. The imagery practice explicitly links the sensory input of imagery to a word.

Let's look in on Miss Billie and Chip. She is overlapping object imagery, receptive and expressive play, and structure word reinforcement. Now she is about to extend to receptive practice with the *Picturing Vocabulary!* Cards.

Receptive Practice with Picturing Vocabulary! Cards

Billie: "Let's play a new game."

Chip: He watches as she puts three *Picturing Vocabulary!* Cards on the table in front of him: a horse, a pig, and a duck.

Billie: "Here are three pictures of farm animals. Find and touch the horse picture."

Chip: He touches the picture of the horse.

Billie: "Right. Thumbs-up! That is the picture of a horse. Touch the picture of a duck."

Chip: He touches the picture of a duck.

Billie: "Are you right or wrong? Give me a thumbs-up or down."

Chip: "Right." He does a thumbs-up.

They do a few more and then Miss Billie changes the task just a little bit.

Billie: "Here are three more cards. I'll say a word. You picture it. Then find the card that matches your picture and put it to sleep."

Billie: "Dog. Put that card to sleep."

Chip: He turns over the picture card of the yellow dog.

Billie: "ZZZZZ. The dog card is sleeping. Now put this one to sleep. Cat."

They do this activity a few times and then overlap to expressive practice.

Lesson Summary:
Receptive Practice with Picturing Vocabulary! Cards

- Teacher says the name of one card.
- Teacher encourages the student to picture the word.
- Student identifies the word by touching the card.
- Student puts the card to "sleep."

SAMPLE LESSON

Expressive Practice with Picturing Vocabulary! Cards

Billie: "This time I touch a card and you tell me what it is." She puts out four cards: duck, horse, pig, and dog. "What is this?" She touches the pig card.

Chip: "Pig."

Billie: "Great! Picture the pig and put the card to sleep."

Chip: He turns the pig card over.

They practice a while longer and then she changes the activity a little bit to keep Chip's attention and energy.

Billie: "Now let's wake up these cards! Turn a card over. Tell me what it is."

Chip: Turning over the truck card, he says, "Truck."

They practice a little while longer and then she changes the activity a little bit more...

Billie: "They are all awake now. Here are some more cards. You touch a card. Tell me what it is."

Chip: He touches the elephant picture card, then doesn't say anything.

Billie: "Good job. You touched this card. Is it a cat or an elephant?"

Chip: He smiles, appearing relieved. "Elephant!"

Billie: "Great. Picture that elephant."

Lesson Summary:
Expressive Practice with Picturing Vocabulary! Cards

- Teacher puts out *Picturing Vocabulary!* Cards.
- Teacher touches a card.
- Student says the name of the card.
- Teacher encourages the student to picture the word.
- Student puts the card to "sleep" and "wakes" it up by naming it.

Picture Imagery Practice

Extend the use of the *Picturing Vocabulary!* Cards to directly stimulate imagery. Show the student a card, take it away, and ask him to picture it and then name it.

Miss Billie is aware that Chip may not be imaging vividly and he may not be able to verbalize the details of what he pictures. She asks him to tell her what he saw and pictured. Then she will prompt him to add the color of the object (something Chip has been successfully doing in previous lessons).

The stimulation with picture vocabulary cards has moved from the category of animals to the category of food.

SAMPLE LESSON

Picture Imagery Practice

Billie: "Here is a new game with your picture cards. I'll show you a card. Then I'll hide it. You tell me what it was. Like this." She holds up a card, takes it away, and then says its name.

Billie: "Now it is your turn." She holds up the card of a big red apple for about two seconds. "Close your eyes and picture that." She takes the card away. "Now tell me what it was."

Chip: He didn't shut his eyes. "Apple."

Billie: "Great! It was an apple. What color was the apple? Can you picture that?"

Chip: He is silent.

Billie: "Let me show it to you again. Don't say anything until I take the card away. Here it is." She shows it to him for another two seconds and then takes it away. "Was it a red apple or a green apple?"

Chip: "Red apple."

They played that game for a while and then Miss Billie changed the activity a little bit.

Lesson Summary:
Picture Imagery Practice

- Teacher shows a *Picturing Vocabulary!* Card to the student for approximately two seconds.
- Teacher takes the card away.
- Student recalls his imagery and names the card.
- Teacher asks for specifics like *color, size,* or *movement.*
- Teacher may show the card again to stimulate imagery-recall for details.

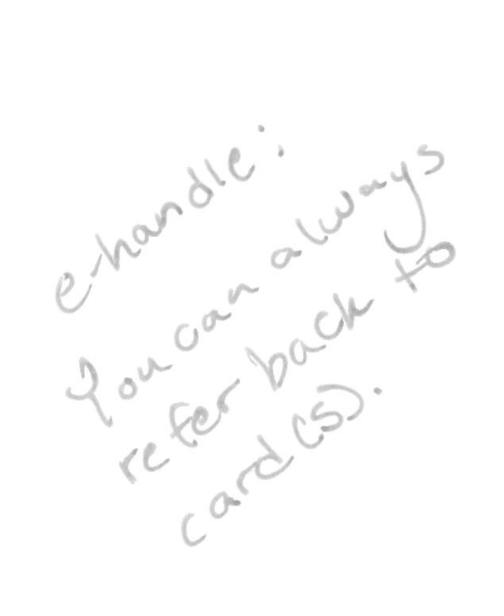

SAMPLE LESSON

Take a Step for Picture Imagery Practice

Billie: "This time, you can stand up over there and take a step toward me." She has Chip stand about six feet away from her. "Here is a new card." She holds up the card with the purple grapes. "Picture that." She takes it away. "What did you picture?"

Chip: "Grapes."

Billie: "Right! Take a step!"

Chip: He takes a step.

Billie: "Were they green grapes or purple grapes?"

Chip: "Purple."

Billie: "Right again! Take another step."

Chip: Smiling, he takes a step.

Billie: "You can jump toward me if you tell me *purple grapes*, two words."

Chip: "Purple grapes."

Billie: "Jump as far as you can toward me!"

Lesson Summary:
Take a Step for Picture Imagery Practice

- Student stands a few feet away from the teacher.
- Teacher shows a *Picturing Vocabulary!* Card to the student for approximately two seconds.
- Teacher takes the card away.
- Student recalls his imagery and names the card.
- If accurate, the student takes a step.
- Teacher asks for specifics like *color, shape,* or *size.*
- Student takes additional steps if he can picture/recall details.
- Teacher may show the card again to stimulate imagery-recall for details.

Words in Categories

As single-word imagery increases with the *Picturing Vocabulary!* Cards, the instruction overlaps to single-word imagery for words within categories. The goal is for your student to create mental representations for relationships of words within categories. In the animal category for example, the animals all have ears, eyes, noses, and legs. Given that our students have difficulty with comprehension and expression, you do not expect to explain the categories to him. Instead, develop imagery and language for the words, exposing him to the detail in the categories.

Here are Miss Billie and Chip, overlapping to relationships within categories. While there are numerous picture vocabulary books on the market, she is using *My Little Word Book,* as it has very simple photographs in basic categories. She could also use the *Picturing Vocabulary!* Book or the *Scholastic First Picture Dictionary.*

SAMPLE LESSON

Receptive Practice for Vocabulary within Categories

Billie: "Here is a page with lots of animals." She shows him the farm animal page in a picture vocabulary book. "They all live on a farm. I'm going to say an animal. You picture it and then find it! Point to the picture of the goose."

Chip: He points to the goose.

Billie: "Great. Let's put a Magic Stone on the goose. Find the cow."

Chip: He points to the cow. She hands him a stone and he puts it on the cow.

Billie: "Good job. When we are done you get to have all the stones you put on the picture. Find the horse."

Chip: He puts a stone on the horse.

Billie: "Let's look at something about all the animals you have put a stone on...they all have legs." She gives the stones to Chip and they look at the legs, then the ears and the eyes. They only look and touch them together, she doesn't ask him to respond or visualize. Her goal is to start some exposure to detail within a category.

Chip: He puts stones on the legs of the animals.

Billie: "Let's play some more. Find the duck and put a stone on it."

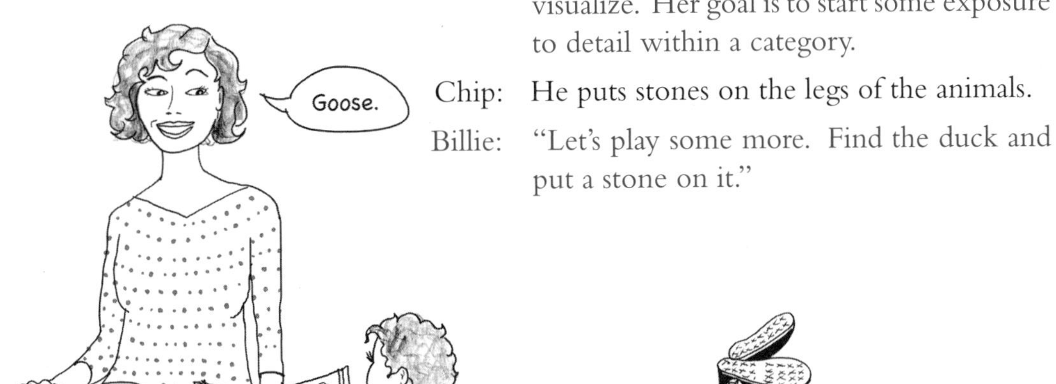

Lesson Summary:
Receptive Practice for Vocabulary within Categories

- Teacher introduces the student to categories of words.
- Teacher names a picture within the category.
- Teacher encourages the student to picture the word.
- Student touches the picture of the word, putting a Magic Stone on it.
- Teacher names the common attributes in the category (such as farm animals have legs, eyes, and ears).
- Student touches or puts a stone on the attribute.

SAMPLE LESSON

Expressive Practice for Vocabulary within Categories

Billie: "Now I'm going to point and you say the name. Then put a stone on it. Remember, you keep all the stones you put on the picture." She points to the goat. "Is this a goat or a cat?"

Chip: "Goat!" Smiling, he puts a stone on the goat.

Billie: "Super. How about this one?"

Chip: "Horse." He puts a stone on the horse.

Billie: "Wow! Great! Picture that horse. What is this on the horse?" She touches his ears. "A leg or an ear?"

Lesson Summary:
Expressive Practice for Vocabulary within Categories

- Teacher touches the picture within the category.
- Student names the picture.
- Student puts a Magic Stone on the picture, if named correctly.
- Teacher names the common attributes of the pictures in the category.
- Teacher touches an attribute and the student names it.
- Teacher refers to imagery.

As the student experiences success with the little steps of receptive and expressive practice for vocabulary and categories, extend the practice to direct stimulation of imagery. All the little steps are a preface for the direct stimulation of imagery.

SAMPLE LESSON

Imagery Practice for Vocabulary within Categories

Billie: "Let's see how many animals you can picture after I hide the book." She points to her head while she is talking. Then she holds up a page in a picture vocabulary book, letting him look at it for a few seconds. Then she hides the book.

Billie: "How many animals can you still picture in your head? I'll give you a stone for each one."

Chip: Looking at Miss Billie, Chip slowly starts to name some of the animals. "Horse. Cow. Cat. Goat."

Billie: "Great!" She watches him closely for signs of imagery. His eyes go up, indicating he is accessing imagery. He is dual coding.

Billie: "Look how many you got!" She shows him the page and together they point and say all of the animals that he was able to name and then together they point and say all the animals that he missed.

Lesson Summary:
Imagery Practice for Vocabulary within Categories

- Teacher shows a page of pictures to the student for approximately two to four seconds.
- Student recalls his imagery and names as many pictures as he can from the page.
- Teacher looks for signs that the student is imaging language.
- Teacher shows the student the page again.
- Teacher and the student point and name the pictures not imaged and recalled.

Magic Window and Magic Glass

The Magic Window and Magic Glass are additional little steps for the identification, categorization, and extension of oral vocabulary. The Magic Window isolates specific pictures within a category—the parts of the bigger whole.

The Magic Window included in the *Talkies* Kit has a square hole cut out in the middle. This "window" is placed on a picture vocabulary card, or on various pictures on a page in a picture vocabulary book. Using the Picture Structure Words, your student begins to discern details about a picture, a word.

Watch Miss Billie use the Magic Window and Picture Structure Words to help Chip get details for each picture/word. She moves from receptive practice to expressive practice and finally to imagery practice.

In the following lesson, Miss Billie chooses the page of words in the food category.

SAMPLE LESSON

Receptive Practice with Magic Window and Picture Structure Words

Billie: "Here is a page with food. And here is your Magic Window." She shows it to Chip, calling his attention to the window part, the hole.

Chip: He feels the hole and puts it up to his face, looking through it at her.

Billie: "The Magic Window goes round and round." She moves it around the page of food pictures. "Where will it stop? You say stop and then we'll see what the window lands on."

Chip: "Stop."

Billie: "Look through the Magic Window. What is in there? I'll say what I see and you give me thumbs-up or down. I see an apple."

Chip: He gives a thumbs-up.

Billie: "Great. I can picture that apple. Now let's use our structure words." She puts the *what*, *color*, and *shape* Picture Structure Words on the table. "Let's check through these cards and you put them to sleep if I am right."

Billie: "This is our *what* structure word. This is an apple." She touches the apple picture in the Magic Window. "If I am right, put the *what* structure word to sleep."

Chip: He turns over the *what* structure word and gives a thumbs-up.

Billie: "Right. It is an apple. You're a good teacher. Let's do the *color* structure word.

	Touch that card for me." Chip touches the *color* structure word card. "Turn the card over if I am right. The apple is red."
Chip:	He turns over the *color* structure word and he gives a thumbs-up.
Billie:	"Great. I was right. We have one more structure word card to turn over, *shape*."

They play with the Magic Window for a while and then Miss Billie overlaps to expressive practice.

Lesson Summary:

Receptive Practice with Magic Window and Picture Structure Words

- Teacher introduces the student to Magic Window.
- Teacher moves the Magic Window around on a page.
- Teacher names the picture in the hole of the Magic Window.
- Student gives thumbs-up or thumbs-down gesture.
- Teacher and the student check through the structure words.
- Student puts the structure word cards to "sleep" if teacher names that specific attribute of the picture.
- Teacher may discuss and name the common attributes in the category.

SAMPLE LESSON

Expressive Practice with Magic Window and Picture Structure Words

Billie:	"This time you get to move the window around and you tell me what you see."
Chip:	He moves the window around and lands on the lemon.
Billie:	"Tell me what you see through your Magic Window."

Chip: "Lemon."

Billie: "Great. Let's go through these structure words. You tell me more about the lemon." She puts the *what*, *color*, *size*, and *shape* cards on the table, touching the *color* card.

Chip: "Yellow."

Billie: "Great. The lemon is yellow. I can picture it. Turn over the *color* card and let's keep going."

Lesson Summary:

Expressive Practice with Magic Window and Picture Structure Words

- Teacher moves the Magic Window around on a page.
- Student names the picture in the hole of the Magic Window.
- Student checks through the structure words.
- Student puts the structure word cards to "sleep" as he verbalizes a specific attribute of the picture.
- Teacher may discuss and name the common attributes in the category.
- Teacher continues to refer to imagery.

The Magic Glass, also included in the *Talkies* Kit, is a small magnifying glass that is similar to the Magic Window in use. As with the Magic Window, the Magic Glass can be used with the *Picturing Vocabulary!* Cards or a picture vocabulary book (to develop recognition of attributes within a category).

In the following lesson, Miss Billie uses a picture vocabulary book. This time, though, Chip is going to look through the Magic Glass, which will bring details of the picture into focus.

SAMPLE LESSON

Receptive Practice with Magic Glass

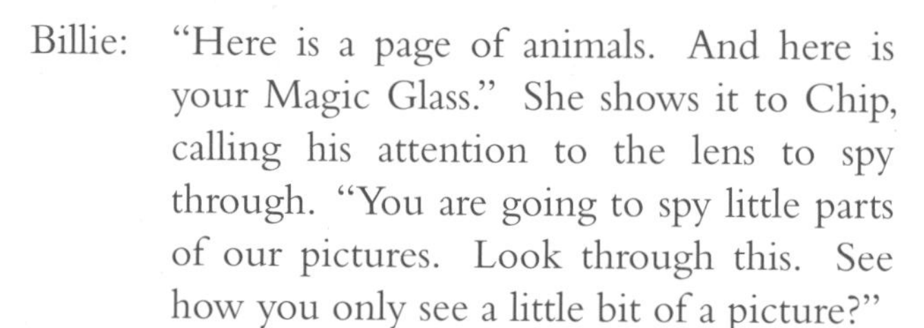

Billie: "Here is a page of animals. And here is your Magic Glass." She shows it to Chip, calling his attention to the lens to spy through. "You are going to spy little parts of our pictures. Look through this. See how you only see a little bit of a picture?"

Chip: He looks through the Magic Glass.

Billie: "Here is the horse picture. Let's use the Magic Glass to look at a little part of the horse." She puts the glass on the head of the horse.

Chip: He looks at the horse through the glass.

Billie: "This is the horse and this is his eye. Give me thumbs-up or down."

Chip: "Right." He gives a thumbs-up.

That's his eye.

Right.

She continues the receptive practice, talking about picturing and calling attention to other eyes in the page of animals.

Lesson Summary:
Receptive Practice with Magic Glass

- Teacher introduces the student to Magic Glass.
- Teacher moves the Magic Glass around on a picture.
- Teacher names the picture in the lens of the Magic Glass.
- Student gives thumbs-up or thumbs-down gesture.
- Teacher and the student may check through the structure words.
- Student puts the structure word cards to "sleep" if the teacher names that specific attribute of the picture.

They do only a little bit of receptive practice, just to get used to the task, and then, because he has been doing so well with other expressive tasks, Miss Billie spends the majority of their time on expressive and imagery practice. She uses the structure words for details when she feels he needs them. In the following lesson, Miss Billie extends the Magic Glass to expressive practice.

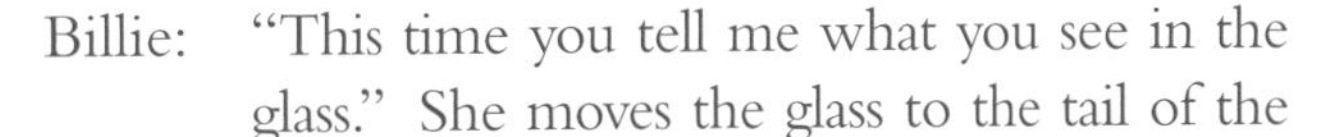

SAMPLE LESSON

Expressive Practice with Magic Glass

Billie: "This time you tell me what you see in the glass." She moves the glass to the tail of the horse in the farm animal category. "What do you see? Is that his tail or his head?"

Chip: "Tail."

Billie: "Great. Tell me more. Is it a brown tail or a black tail?"

Chip: "Brown."

Miss Billie focuses on the parts/words in a category that are fundamental to the category. For example, for the animal category, she focuses on the tail, the ears, the eyes, the legs, etc.

They play with the Magic Glass for a while and then Miss Billie extends the lesson to directly stimulate imagery.

Lesson Summary:
Expressive Practice with Magic Glass

- Student moves the Magic Glass around on a picture.
- Student names the picture in the lens of the Magic Glass.
- Student may check through the structure words.
- Teacher names common attributes in a category.

Chip is ready to start directly practicing imagery with the Magic Glass. As in previous imagery practice, the stimulation is based on recall of imagery rather than created imagery.

SAMPLE LESSON

Imagery Practice with Magic Glass

Billie: "I'll put the Glass on the picture. Then I'll take the Glass away and cover up the picture. Tell me what you pictured." She moves the Glass to the legs of the cow, takes it away, and then covers the cow up. "What do you picture?"

Chip: "Legs."

Billie: "Great. Those were legs. Let's see what those legs were on." She shows him the cow.

Chip: "Cow."

Billie: "Right. Look how many legs are on this page! These animals all have legs! Let's do some more."

Lesson Summary:
Imagery Practice with Magic Glass

- Teacher puts the Magic Glass on a part of a picture for approximately two seconds.
- Student recalls his imagery and names what he recalls (images).
- Teacher looks for signs that the student is accessing imagery.
- Teacher shows the student the picture and they discuss details of the picture that they may have missed.

Magic Bag for Imagery and Verbalization

In the Magic Bag little step, your student solves a mystery that directly and explicitly stimulates imagery and verbalization from kinesthetic input. The student reaches into the Magic Bag, feels a toy, visualizes it, and then tells you what he is feeling and picturing. To facilitate success, there are initially only two or three toys in the bag and they have wide contrasts, such as a ball and a car, rather than a car and a truck. Since you can't see in the bag either, your student knows he has to verbalize enough for you to picture or guess the toy. He learns that he needs to give more detail, such as "Animal, four legs, tail, ears, nose..." to help your imagery.

The kinesthetic sensory input transfers to imagery, which transfers to verbalization—a perfect integration of the sensory dominos moving up and down, working with each other.

Don't do receptive and expressive practice with the Magic Bag unless they are needed. If your student has been doing fairly well with imagery in the Magic Window and Magic Glass practice, move directly to imagery practice with the Magic Bag.

SAMPLE LESSON

Imagery Practice with Magic Bag: Student Uses Magic Hands to Feel, Image, and Describe

Billie: "Here is a Magic Bag! There are toys in it. But you can't see them. Put your magic hands in the bag and feel the toys." She hands him the Magic Bag, which has a little ball, a big ball, and a little teddy bear.

Chip: Excited, he puts his hands in the bag, feeling the toys.

Billie: "Choose one toy to feel. Let your magic hands give you a picture of the toy. Then tell me what you are picturing. I'm going to picture it too."

Chip: He feels around, more excited. "Ball."

Billie: "Great! It is a ball. Let your magic hands help you picture if it is a big ball or a little ball."

Chip: "Little ball."

Billie: "What is the shape of the ball, round or square? Feel it with your magic hands."

Chip: He feels inside the bag, eyes up. "Round! It round." He flashes a big smile.

Billie: "Okay. Get it out! Let's see if your picture and your words matched what is in the bag."

Chip: He gets out the ball he was feeling.

Billie: "Great job! You get three points for that!" She has been giving him points on a paper without saying, "use your words," which can be a negative verbal command, given his past. Instead, she makes it obvious she gives him a point every time he says a word. "Your magic hands helped you picture in your mind, like this." She re-sets the climate for him by quickly drawing a head with a thought bubble, and then puts a ball in the bubble.

They play with the Magic Bag for a while and then Miss Billie changes the lesson just a little bit more.

Lesson Summary:

Imagery Practice with Magic Bag: Student Uses Magic Hands to Feel, Image, and Describe

- Teacher puts two or three toys in the Magic Bag.
- Student feels inside the bag.
- Student feels, images, and names the toy he chooses to describe.
- Teacher looks for signs that the student is accessing imagery.
- Student takes the toy he described out of the bag to see if he was right or wrong.

In the next lesson, Miss Billie changes the stimulation just a little bit keeping Chip's attention so she can to continue to stimulate his imagery.

SAMPLE LESSON

Imagery Practice with Magic Bag: Teacher Describes and Student Images and Guesses the Name

Billie: "I'll reach in the bag and tell you what I'm feeling and picturing. You win if you can tell me what it is!" She reaches in the bag they have just been using, increasing Chip's chances for success. The bag has a red car, a plastic cow, and a ball.

Billie: "My magic hands are helping me picture something hard with four wheels, and—"

Chip: He jumps up. "Red car! It a red car."

Billie: "Let's see!" She gets the car out of the bag. "Wow! Great picturing!"

Chip: He smiles and jumps around.

Billie: "You knew it was a red car because you pictured it red. You saw the red car just a little bit ago. You remembered the color because you pictured it!"

Lesson Summary:
Imagery Practice with Magic Bag: Teacher Describes and Student Images and Guesses the Name

- Teacher feels inside the Magic Bag.
- Teacher feels, visualizes, and verbalizes.
- Teacher looks for signs that the student is imaging.
- Student guesses the name of the toy.
- Teacher gets the toy she described out of the bag and the student gets to see if he was right or wrong.

In the lesson below, Miss Billie changes the stimulation just a little bit more. This time they sit on the floor.

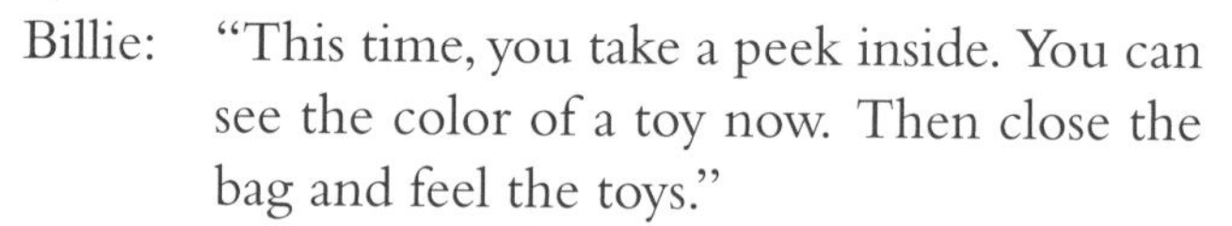

Imagery Practice with Magic Bag: Student Peeks Inside, Images, and Describes

Billie: "This time, you take a peek inside. You can see the color of a toy now. Then close the bag and feel the toys."

Chip: Smiling, he eagerly looks inside the Magic Bag. There are three new toys in the bag, this time with finer contrasts: a green car, a blue airplane, and a red ball. He looks closely at the toy he chooses to tell about, and then closes the bag.

Billie: "Help me picture and guess what you are feeling. Don't tell me the name of the toy. Just tell me things like color and size, hard or soft, big or little."

Chip: "Blue."

Billie: "Hmmm. Blue. A blue truck."

Chip: "No."

Billie: "Does it have wheels?"

Chip: Still feeling, he smiles. "No."

Billie: "Help me! Give me more information. Is it round?"

Chip: He smiles. "No. Hard. Blue. It hard blue."

Billie: "Hmmm. It is hard and blue. It has no wheels. A ball?"

Chip: He laughs out loud. "No!"

Billie: "Okay. I need more help! Is it a boat? A boat has no wheels and it is hard."

Chip: "No! It fly."

Billie: "It can fly? Oh, I know. Your words made me picture it. Is it a blue airplane?"

Chip: "Yes! It blue airplane."

Billie: "Get it out. Let's look at it."

Chip: He gets the blue airplane out of the bag, smiling. Delighted, he and Miss Billie count all the points he got for that little lesson.

Lesson Summary:
Imagery Practice with Magic Bag: Student Peeks Inside, Images, and Describes

- Student peeks inside the Magic Bag, choosing a toy to describe.
- Student describes the toy with details to help the teacher picture and guess the name of the toy.
- Teacher looks for signs that the student is imaging.
- Teacher describes what the student's words made her picture.
- Teacher guesses the name of the toy.
- Student gets the toy out of the bag to show the teacher if she is right or wrong.

Vocabulary Tracking

The *Picturing Vocabulary!* Tracking Chart presents each of the words from the *Picturing Vocabulary!* Cards for practice and imagery. The chart has pictures of common words and boxes for noting if a word is being practiced or has been learned. As you practice the word, by pointing to it and asking your student to tell you what it is, give him a check mark on the chart. When your student can name the word quickly without prompting, make a large check mark or let him paste a star next to the word.

Error Handling

When doing the various lessons in Talking Words, remember to use responding to the response for any incorrect responses. To remind you, here are the principles of error handling: 1) note the student's response, 2) find a spot in the student's response from which to positively engage him, 3) help him analyze his response, and 4) help him compare his response to the stimulus.

In the lesson below, Chip says the wrong color for lemon, though he knows his colors. Notice that even if Miss Billie feels pressured for time, she knows better than to say, "No, Chip. The lemon is not red, it is yellow." Telling a student "no" and then giving the answer serves little purpose, not even saving time. A negative response may cause him to feel less enthusiastic about interacting with her, and the next time she questions him he may not be as eager to respond. Giving him the answer doesn't help him learn to analyze and compare his response to the stimulus.

Along with the specific stimulation in *Talkies*, you are teaching your student to learn to learn. Let's watch Miss Billie note Chip's response, engage with him on a positive, and then help him compare his response to the stimulus.

SAMPLE LESSON

Expressive Practice with Magic Window and Picture Structure Words

ERROR: Chip says the wrong color for the lemon.

Billie: "This time you get to move the window around and you tell me what you see."

Chip: He moves the window around and lands on a lemon.

Billie: "Tell me what you see through your Magic Window."

Chip: "Red."

Billie: "Good. You told me a color. You said the color is red. Let's check some colors." She puts red, yellow, and purple colored squares on the table. "I'm going to put a Magic

	Stone on each square and you get the stone if you can find the color. Find *red*."
Chip:	He touches the red square and says, "Red."
Billie:	"Great. Take the stone. Find *yellow*."
Chip:	"Yellow." He touches yellow square and takes the stone.
Billie:	"Right. That is yellow. You said this was red." She points to the yellow lemon.
Chip:	"This yellow. It not red!"

Chip is now beginning to talk in fuller sentences, but Miss Billie consistently restates his sentence as a complete sentence. She has purposefully avoided telling him to "talk." She doesn't say, "Use your words," instead she gives him immediate rewards and praise when he does talk or use words.

Practice and Pacing

Remember to overlap steps to keep the energy and attention of your student while also moving toward your goal. It cannot be said enough, these are little steps within larger steps, and our students need the little steps to keep their attention, reinforce the sensory stimulation, and move forward.

At this level of *Talkies*, you may be overlapping numerous steps, some from the Sensory-Language Play step and some from this Talking Words step. Don't move too slowly. In teaching individuals to do the *Lindamood Phoneme Sequencing (LiPS) Program*, *Seeing Stars*, *V/V*, and *Talkies*, nearly everyone tends to move too slow rather than too fast! You can always return to a previous step, so do not look for mastery before you overlap to another step. If your student is beginning to use two or more words in a sentence, overlap to the next step, Talking Sentences.

Summary: Step 3 Talking Words

Goal: Develop imagery for oral vocabulary and basic concepts, and increase word retrieval for expressive language.

1. Introduce Picture Structure Words

- Teacher names a structure word.
- Student finds and touches the appropriate card.
- Teacher concretizes the structure word with toys, movements, and contrast.

2. Receptive Practice with *Picturing Vocabulary!* Cards

- Teacher says the name of one card.
- Teacher encourages the student to picture the word.
- Student identifies the word by touching the card.
- Student puts the card to "sleep."

3. Expressive Practice with *Picturing Vocabulary!* Cards

- Teacher puts out the *Picturing Vocabulary!* Cards.
- Teacher touches a card.

- Student says the name of the card.
- Teacher encourages the student to picture the word.
- Student puts the card to "sleep" and "wakes" it up by naming it.

4. Picture Imagery Practice

- Teacher shows a *Picturing Vocabulary!* Card to the student for approximately two seconds.
- Teacher takes the card away.
- Student recalls his imagery and names the card.
- Teacher asks for specifics like *color, size,* or *movement.*
- Teacher may show the card again to stimulate imagery-recall for details.

5. Take a Step for Picture Imagery Practice

- Student stands a few feet away from the teacher.
- Teacher shows a *Picturing Vocabulary!* Card to the student for approximately two seconds.
- Teacher takes the card away.
- Student recalls his imagery and names the card.
- If accurate, the student takes a step.
- Teacher asks for specifics like *color, shape,* or *size.*
- Student takes additional steps if he can picture/recall details.
- Teacher may show the card again to stimulate imagery-recall for details.

6. Receptive Practice for Vocabulary within Categories

- Teacher introduces the student to categories of words.
- Teacher names a picture within the category.
- Teacher encourages the student to picture the word.

- Student touches the picture of the word, putting a Magic Stone on it.
- Teacher names the common attributes in the category (such as farm animals have legs, eyes, and ears).
- Student touches or puts a stone on the attribute.

7. Expressive Practice for Vocabulary within Categories

- Teacher touches the picture within the category.
- Student names the picture.
- Student puts a Magic Stone on the picture, if named correctly.
- Teacher names the common attributes of the pictures in the category.
- Teacher touches an attribute and the student names it.
- Teacher refers to imagery.

8. Imagery Practice for Vocabulary within Categories

- Teacher shows a page of pictures to the student for approximately two to four seconds.
- Student recalls his imagery and names as many pictures as he can from the page.
- Teacher looks for signs that the student is imaging language.
- Teacher shows the student the page again.
- Teacher and the student point and name the pictures not imaged and recalled.

9. Receptive Practice with Magic Window and Picture Structure Words

- Teacher introduces the student to Magic Window.
- Teacher moves the Magic Window around on a page.
- Teacher names the picture in the hole of the Magic Window.
- Student gives thumbs-up or thumbs-down gesture.
- Teacher and the student check through the structure words.

- Student puts the structure word cards to "sleep" if teacher names that specific attribute of the picture.
- Teacher may discuss and name the common attributes in the category.

10. Expressive Practice with Magic Window and Picture Structure Words

- Teacher moves the Magic Window around on a page.
- Student names the picture in the hole of the Magic Window.
- Student checks through the structure words.
- Student puts the structure word cards to "sleep" as he verbalizes a specific attribute of the picture.
- Teacher may discuss and name the common attributes in the category.
- Teacher continues to refer to imagery.

11. Receptive Practice with Magic Glass

- Teacher introduces the student to Magic Glass.
- Teacher moves the Magic Glass around on a picture.
- Teacher names the picture in the hole of the Magic Glass.
- Student gives thumbs-up or thumbs-down gesture.
- Teacher and the student may check through the structure words.
- Student puts the structure word cards to "sleep" if the teacher names that specific attribute of the picture.

12. Expressive Practice with Magic Glass

- Student moves the Magic Glass around on a picture.
- Student names the picture in the hole of the Magic Glass.
- Student may check through the structure words.
- Teacher names common attributes in a category.

13. Imagery Practice with Magic Glass

- Teacher puts the Magic Glass on a part of a picture for approximately two seconds.
- Student recalls his imagery and names what he recalls (images).
- Teacher looks for signs that the student is accessing imagery.
- Teacher shows the student the picture and they discuss details of the picture that they may have missed.

14. Imagery Practice with Magic Bag: Student Uses Magic Hands to Feel, Image, and Describe

- Teacher puts two or three toys in the Magic Bag.
- Student feels inside the bag.
- Student feels, images, and names the toy he chooses to describe.
- Teacher looks for signs that the student is accessing imagery.
- Student takes the toy he described out of the bag to see if he was right or wrong.

15. Imagery Practice with Magic Bag: Teacher Describes and Student Images and Guesses the Name

- Teacher feels inside the Magic Bag.
- Teacher feels, visualizes, and verbalizes.
- Teacher looks for signs that the student is imaging.
- Student guesses the name of the toy.
- Teacher gets the toy she described out of the bag and the student gets to see if he was right or wrong.

16. Imagery Practice with Magic Bag: Student Peeks Inside, Images, and Describes

- Student peeks inside the Magic Bag, choosing a toy to describe.
- Student describes the toy with details to help the teacher picture and guess the name of the toy.
- Teacher looks for signs that the student is imaging.
- Teacher describes what the student's words made her picture.
- Teacher guesses the name of the toy.
- Student gets the toy out of the bag to show the teacher if she is right or wrong.

Group Instruction

The biggest challenge in group instruction is keeping the attention of each student. Manage your group with the thumbs-up or thumbs-down gesture and reward students randomly for participating.

☞ Introduce the Picture Structure Words to a group, using the same steps as in individual instruction, making sure to get all the students involved. For example, when introducing *movement* and *color,* have the group participate in movements such as hopping around the room or have the group point out items of a particular color. Randomly, not round robin, encourage the whole group to respond with thumbs-up or thumbs-down to each student's response.

☞ In receptive and expressive practice with the picture cards, continue to keep the whole group participating and responding in turn. Ask one student to find one picture and the next to find another, while those students not directly involved respond with thumbs-up or thumbs-down gestures. This activity easily turns into a fun game that allows you to keep "score" of which students are able to identify and respond correctly to the picture cards.

Picture Imagery Practice is done cooperatively with one object shown to the whole group. Once all students have closed their eyes, each student gets a chance to say one thing about what they imaged.

When you begin to work on vocabulary within categories, have the students take turns finding pictures that would fit into the chosen category.

In Expressive Practice and Imagery Practice with a picture vocabulary book, students take turns identifying and recalling objects within the category.

- The Magic Window steps need to be modified slightly for small or large group instruction. Have one student find and name the object in the window and let the other students use structure words to help describe it. Then have another student guide the window and name the next object. Likewise, the students should take turns using the Magic Glass, with one student identifying the part and others verbalizing its descriptive details. The thumbs-up or thumbs-down gesture keeps other students involved when one is taking a turn.

- The Magic Bag exercises are played like a guessing game. Students take turns feeling the objects in the bag and using the structure words to describe them while you and the others guess their identity. Imagery Practice is done in a similar manner. As you describe the object in the bag, the students take turns guessing what it is.

Talking Sentences

We are now at the heart of *Talkies*—Talking Sentences. Here the student is given direct stimulation in verbalizing two- to seven-word sentences. The goal is to develop imagery and increase the complexity and length of sentences in expressive language. The stimulation uses manipulatives and techniques to explicitly develop imagery and verbalization for sentences with a subject and a verb to sentences with adjectives, articles, connectors, prepositions, and objects.

The heart of the *V/V* program is the Sentence by Sentence step, a perceptual threshold where the student moves from parts to a whole—*isolated sentences to a whole concept*. The heart of *Talkies* is Talking Sentences, another perceptual threshold where the student also moves from parts to a whole—*isolated words to a whole sentence*. The hearts of both *Talkies* and *V/V* are the instructional steps that develop the student's ability to bring parts to a whole.

In this step, the conscious integration of imagery and language is facilitated with the use of concrete objects (toys) and picture cards on colored squares. In Sentence by Sentence *V/V*, the colored squares represent *each sentence* in a paragraph. In *Talkies*, the colored squares represent *each word* in a sentence. *Word by word, a sentence is represented, manipulated, and expressed.*

A Look at Chip Now

As we look in with Miss Billie and Chip, he is beginning his fifth week of *Talkies*. He trusts Miss Billie, shows evidence of reciprocity, laughs often, and often runs into the room for his lessons. His mother reports that he seems to be less removed from conversation and is talking a little more at home.

Miss Billie continues to closely watch and listen to Chip and what she notes thrills her. He is beginning to demonstrate outward signs of imagery. Occasionally, his eyes go up to create a mental representation and he doesn't have that blank look of language going in and out without a sensory connection.

Talking in Two-Word Sentences

This little step begins with the simplest sentence, a noun and a verb. The words are concretized on the colored squares with toys and picture cards. A toy or picture card is used for the noun and placed on the first colored square to concretize the subject (noun) in the sentence, providing a recall-stimulus. The *Talkies* Movement Cards for basic actions such as *run*, *walk*, *jump*, *hop*, and *swim* are placed on the second colored square and likewise concretize the verb and provide a recall-stimulus. Immediately after the card has been placed on the square, turn it over to hide the illustration from view. Mental imagery for the word within the context of the sentence should replace the illustration. As the lessons progress, the concrete objects and picture cards are removed, leaving the colored squares to represent both imagery and language.

One word is changed at a time to provide the child with a safe, repetitive imagery-language experience. He sees and feels the rhythm of language while saying and touching each word in the two-word sentence. As a word changes, the colored square also changes whether or not the square has been concretized with an object or a card.

The *Talkies* Movement Cards should be introduced and practiced as you did the *Picturing Vocabulary!* Cards. It is important that the student can identify the movement in the card prior to using it on a colored square.

Let's visit Miss Billie and Chip as she introduces him to the new task of using colored squares and toys to create sentences. Chip has just completed a session that included picture vocabulary cards and imagery practice in Magic Window, Magic Glass, and Magic Bag.

In the lesson below, the two-word sentence *Chip runs* has two colored squares with a picture of Chip on the first colored square and a Movement Card on the second square.

SAMPLE LESSON

Talking Two-Word Sentences with Teacher Generating the Change

Billie: "We are going to use these colored squares to show words we say. Here is the first word I'm going to say. The word is *Chip*. Find a picture of the word." She puts out two picture cards on the table, one of Chip and one of a duck.

Chip: "This." He points to the picture of himself, smiling.

Billie: "Right! Now take my hand. Let's count how many words I say. *Chip runs.*" Miss Billie makes a fist and extends a finger every time she taps the table. Then they count her fingers. "How many words?"

Chip: "Two."

Billie: "Yes! Two words. *Chip runs*. Let's put out two of these colored squares." She repeats the words as she puts out each square. "Touch each square and say it with me."

Chip: "Chip runs." He touches each square as he says it.

Billie: "Good job. Put your picture on the square that says your name. Let's do it together again." They touch the squares and say the sentence again.

Chip: He successfully places his picture on the first colored square.

Billie: "Good job. Now let's find a card that shows the word *run*." She places two Movement Cards (previously introduced and practiced) with wide contrast in front of Chip, *run* and *swim*. "Which card shows what it looks like to run?"

Chip: He chooses the card showing *run*. "Run. This is run."

Billie: "Oh, so good. I didn't even have to ask you to say the word. Put it on this square." She touches the second square.

Chip: He places the *run* card on the second colored square. "Run."

Billie: "Yup. Get two stones." She turns the Movement Card over. "Take my hand and we'll say the sentence." Holding Chip's hand, Miss Billie and Chip touch each colored square as they say each word. "*Chip runs*. Touch each square and say it by yourself."

Chip: "Chip runs." He touches each colored square as he says the words, smiling and happy with himself.

Billie: "Great job. Now you can do what the sentence says! Run to the door and back."

Chip: Excited, Chip jumps up and runs to the door and back again.

Billie: "Great! Now, we'll change just one word. *Chip runs*." She takes his hand and helps him touch and say each word in the old and the new sentence. "*Chip jumps*. Does *Chip* change?"

Chip: "No."

Billie: "Does *run* change? *Chip jumps*. What are you picturing Chip doing? Does he run or jump?"

Chip: "Jump. Chip jumps."

Billie: "Right. So we take out this square and the card. We get a new square. Now what card do we need to show *jump*?" She has two cards for him to choose from, *jump* and *swim*.

Chip: "Jump." He chooses the *jump* Movement Card.

Billie: "Right! Thumbs-up. Let's touch those words now, and say each of them. *Chip jumps*." They touch and say the words together.

Chip: "Chip jumps."

Billie: "Right. Let's take off your picture." She removes it from the first colored square. "This will still say *Chip jumps*. But now we'll just picture *Chip* in our minds! Touch the squares and say the words with me again, picturing *Chip*."

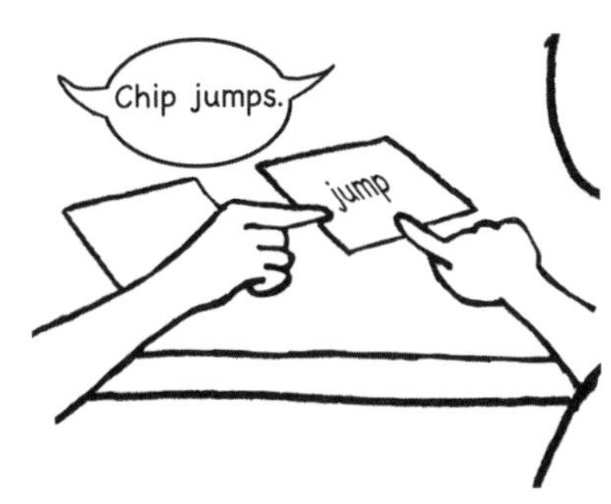

Chip: "Chip jumps." Miss Billie says it with him as she directs his hand to each colored square.

Billie: "Great. Now close your eyes and picture yourself jumping."

Chip: He sort of squints his eyes, just for a second.

Billie: "Picture *Chip jumps*. Now do it!"

Chip: He gets up and jumps up and down, smiling.

Billie: "So good! Those words made you picture jumping and then you jumped. Let's change it again. This one says *Chip jumps*.' Let's make it say *Cow jumps*. Which word changed?"

Chip: "Cow jumps." He touches the colored squares as he says the sentence.

Billie: "Right. *Chip* is gone." She removes the first colored square and gets a new one. "We want this to say *Cow jumps*. Get the toy we need to show that." She puts out three toys: a cow, a pig, and a truck.

Chip: "Cow. This cow." He picks up the cow and puts it on the new square.

Billie: "Good job! Say that sentence for me. Touch each word."

Chip: "Chip jumps. No. Cow jumps."

Billie: "Wow! You corrected yourself! A big thumbs-up. Picture the cow jumping. Now take the cow and make her jump around on the table."

Chip: Holding the cow in his hand, he makes her jump around, careful not to disturb his growing pile of stones. Then he does something that thrills Miss Billie, he links the action to the words. "Cow jumps. Cow jumps."

Billie: "That's right! The cow jumps. I'm going to change a word." She replaces the colored square that was under the toy cow with a new square and a toy tiger. "Now let's say this sentence." She starts to take his hand but he starts to talk.

Chip: "Tiger jumps!"

Billie: "Right. This says *Tiger jumps*. Say it again and touch each square so you can feel the words."

Chip: "Tiger jumps." He touches each word in the sentence as he says it.

Billie: "Yes, oh yes. Guess what? Now you can take the tiger and make it jump on the table."

Chip: Smiling, he takes the tiger and makes it jump around the table, again being careful not to bother his pile of stones. "Tiger jumps."

Lesson Summary:

Talking Two-Word Sentences with Teacher Generating the Change

- Teacher creates a sentence with a noun and a verb.
- Language is concretized on colored squares with toys or picture cards.
- Teacher changes one word at a time.
- Teacher starts with a noun on the first square and a Movement Card on the second square.
- Student touches each square and says sentence.
- Teacher changes a word.
- Student touches each square and says the sentence.
- Student changes the square or the square and the card, as appropriate.

Note: The student can choose the toys or cards to match what the teacher says, or the teacher can place the toy or cards on the colored squares and then have the student say the sentence. This is just a tiny change in the activity, but it helps keep the student's attention and energy.

Talking Two-Word Sentences with Student Generating the Change

As Chip progresses through the lessons, he gets to initiate the change, rather than his teacher. He decides what word is changing, makes the change, and verbalizes his sentence.

For example, Chip takes out the colored square and the toy for the subject (noun) in *Tiger jumps* and brings back a new colored square with a new toy, saying, "Dinosaur jumps." *The lesson always ends with the student touching and saying the sentence.*

Lesson Summary:
Talking Two-Word Sentences with Student Generating the Change

- Student chooses an object and a Movement Card and places them on colored squares.
- Student touches each square and says the sentence.
- Student chooses a new object or Movement Card, changing one word in the sentence.
- Student changes the square or the square and card, as appropriate.
- Student touches each square and says the sentence.

Miss Billie and Chip make good progress with two-word sentences, using a toy or card to concretize the noun and the verb. As he improves, she overlaps to only concretizing the noun in the sentence. She is going to stimulate imagery for the verb, the action of the sentence.

Their last sentence was *Pig hops*. Let's listen as Billie changes the activity a little bit.

SAMPLE LESSON

Talking Two-Word Sentences with Imagery for the Verb

Billie: "This time we won't put a card on the second square." She replaces the colored square and the *hop* Movement Card with a new colored square, but with no card on it. "This time you can just imagine this part, picture it." She touches the second square.

Chip: He stares at the new empty colored square.

Billie: "This used to say *Pig hops*. Now it will say *Pig eats*." She takes Chip's hand and they touch the squares, saying the words. *Pig eats.*"

Chip: "Pig eats."

Billie: "Great. Picture the pig eating." She changes the colored square again. "Let's change it again. *Pig eats* changes to *Pig runs.*"

Lesson Summary:
Talking Two-Word Sentences with Imagery for the Verb

- Teacher creates a two-word sentence without concretizing the verb with a Movement Card.
- Student pictures the verb.
- Teacher changes one word in the sentence.
- Student touches each square and says the sentence.
- Student may act out the verb and may take a turn making the changes in the sentence.
- A colored square changes when a word changes.

Talking Two-Word Sentences with Imagery for the Whole Sentence

As the student progresses, the colored squares continue to represent words, but now without objects or picture cards. The squares/words continue to be touched, visualized, and verbalized. With only colored squares to represent language, imagery is directly stimulated. For example, "This time we have no objects or cards. We will picture the words in our minds. *Duck walks.* Picture the duck walking. Now, let's change that to *Duck swims.* Which square has to change? *Duck walks. Duck swims.*"

Duck walks.
Duck swims.

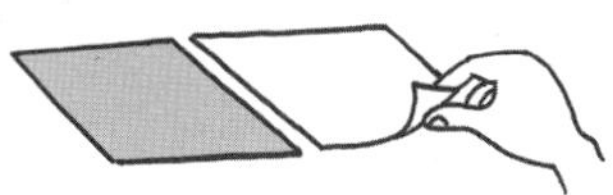

The above instruction stimulates imagery and verbal expression. Do not try to concretize the experience by matching a colored square with some aspect of a word. For example, do not try to use a yellow colored square for *Yellow cat runs* or a green square for *Cat runs up the tree.* It ends in confusion for both the teacher and the student, but more importantly, it may interfere with imagery—the goal of the lesson.

Lesson Summary:
Talking Two-Word Sentences with Imagery for the Whole Sentence

- Teacher creates a sentence without placing objects and cards on the squares.
- Student touches each square and says the sentence.
- Teacher encourages the student to picture.
- Teacher changes one word in the sentence.
- Student touches each square and says the sentence.
- Student may make the change and verbalize the sentence.

Adjectives for a Three-Word Sentence

The basic structure words of *color* and *size* extend the sentence to three words, without the abstraction of articles or connectors. With or without objects or picture cards on the squares, the *color* structure word is added as a familiar and concrete means of extending the student's expressive language and imagery.

For example, placing the previously experienced and established *color* structure word at the beginning of the sentence, the child chooses whatever color he wants. *Dog runs* changes to *Yellow dog runs*. Depending on the level of your student, he may overlap to this step without cards or toys to concretize the words. Or you might overlap to this step when he is still using a toy or a Movement Card.

On the third day of doing Talking Sentences, while also continuing practice with Talking Words, Chip is progressing nicely and it is time to extend the sentence by using some known adjectives. He is moving to three-word sentences with his own imagery concretizing the colored squares. He has created the sentence *Airplane flies*.

SAMPLE LESSON

Adjectives for a Three-Word Sentence

Billie: "Let's add another word! Let me show you. Touch the words and then say the sentence. *Airplane flies.*"

Chip: "Airplane flies."

Billie: "Let's give that airplane a color. Do you want to picture a red airplane or a blue airplane? You choose."

Chip: "Red."

Billie: "Okay. Let's put a new square first." She puts a new colored square in the first position. "*Red airplane flies.* Touch the squares and say it."

Chip: "Red airplane flies."

Billie: "Great job, Chip. Now, picture the red airplane flying. Use your hand to pretend the airplane is flying over my head!"

Chip: He takes his hand and pretends the airplane is flying, standing up and making it fly over Miss Billie's head.

Billie: "Okay, let's keep going. I'll say a new sentence. Change *Red airplane flies* to *Blue airplane flies.* Touch the squares and say, *Red airplane flies.* Now make it say *Blue airplane flies.*"

Chip: "Blue airplane flies." Chip replaces the first colored square with a new square.

Billie: "Super! Picture a blue airplane flying! You're at three words, Chip! We're only going to go up to six or seven words, so you are doing great."

Lesson Summary:
Adjectives for a Three-Word Sentence

- Teacher places a new square and adds an adjective before the noun in the sentence.
- Student touches each square and says the sentence.
- Teacher encourages the student to picture.
- The words may or may not be concretized on the sentence.

Concept Cards for a Three-Word Sentence

As with the structure words, the *Talkies* Concept Cards extend the sentence from two to three words. *Talkies* Concept Cards are modeled after the "Basic Concepts" enumerated by Ann E. Boehm, but they do not cover the complete list. Presented in the order of concreteness, the Concept Cards are: *up, down, on, off, over, under, in, out, first, last, in front, behind, front, back, near,* and *far.* As with the Movement Cards, Concept Cards are introduced and practiced prior to being used within a sentence.

A Concept Card and a colored square are added to the end of the sentence. *Cat runs* becomes *Cat runs up.* The Concept Card is added only to concretize the concept and stimulate recall. After the student has placed the card in the sentence, turn it over. The student should then change his imagery for the word to fit the context of the sentence. That is, you want him to picture the cat running up, not the stick figure from the card. Finally, your student chooses what he wants to picture the cat running up. For example, if he is using a toy cat to concretize the sentence, he verbalizes what he pictures the cat running up and then he acts it out.

Concept Cards for a Three-Word Sentence

Billie: "Let's make another sentence with three words. *Cat runs.* Get those squares."

Chip: He gets two colored squares.

Billie: “Good job. Touch each square and say the sentence. *Cat runs.*”

Chip: “Cat runs.”

Billie: “Great. Let’s have the cat run up or down. Choose either the *up* card or the *down* card.” She puts those two cards on the table.

Chip: “Up.”

Billie: “Good. *Cat runs up.* Put that card where it goes. Does it go at the first part of the sentence?” She puts the card first. “Or does it go last?” She moves the card to last.

Chip: “Cat runs up.” Chip takes the *up* card from Miss Billie and places it last. Miss Billie gets him a colored square to place under the card.

Billie: “Great! The sentence says *Cat runs up.*” She turns the card over so the picture is hidden from view. “You can picture that and you can do that. Picture a cat running up something in this room. Take a toy cat and make it run up what you pictured!”

Chip: He gets a toy cat and makes it run up his leg.

Billie: “Fun! Say your sentence when you do it.”

Chip: “Cat runs up. Cat runs up.”

Billie: “Right! Cat runs up your leg or your arm? Do it again.”

Chip: “Cat runs up leg.”

Lesson Summary:
Concept Cards for a Three-Word Sentence

- The Concept Cards are used at the end of a sentence to modify the verb.
- Student chooses the Concept Card to put on a square.
- Student touches each square and says the sentence.
- Teacher or the student changes a word in the sentence.

Following the same procedure, with either the teacher changing a word or the student changing a word, the sentence changes from *Cat runs up* to *Goat runs up* to *Goat jumps up* to *Goat jumps down*. Expressive language is developed and extended, and concepts are experienced and imaged.

Adding Articles and Connectors

The addition of articles and connectors is introduced at the two-word sentence level, extending the sentence to three words. Given the abstraction of an article or connector, introduce them only after the student is accustomed to three words using an adjective and/or a concept.

Begin with the simplest articles: *the* and *a*. The sentence *Cat runs*, with or without toys/cards, can be changed to *The cat runs*. It is as simple as adding a new colored square at the beginning, and then touching the squares and saying each word in the sentence.

SAMPLE LESSON

Adding Articles and Connectors

Billie: "Get your squares and show me how many words are in *Pig snorts. Snort* is like this." She does a snort sound. "Put your toy pig on one of the squares. Say the sentence to me."

Chip: He puts the toy pig on the first colored square. "Pig snorts." Smiling shyly, Chip snorts.

Billie: "Right. You snorted! Let's add a new word here at the beginning. It is hard to picture, but we use it when we talk. Okay?"

Chip: "Okay."

Billie: "This square says *A*." She puts the square in front of the toy pig. Now the sentence says *A pig snorts*. I'm going to make you a card with the word *A* on it, so we can put it on the square." She writes the letter *A* on a 3x5 card and puts it on the empty square, not expecting him to read it but concretizing the abstraction with a word. She will do the same for *the*. "This says *A*. Say it with me."

Chip: "A."

Billie: "Great! Let's touch each square and say the whole sentence together. *A pig snorts*."

Chip: "A pig snorts." He touches each square as he says each word.

Billie: "Easy, huh? *A pig snorts*. Change that to say *A pig jumps*."

Chip: Taking out the last colored square, Chip brings in a new colored square. "A pig jumps."

Billie: "Good job! Picture the pig jumping. This time it is your turn to make the change. Change the pig to something else and then say the sentence to me."

Lesson Summary:
Adding Articles and Connectors

- Student says a two-word sentence.
- Teacher places a new square to represent the article.
- Teacher uses the *Talkies* Article Cards or prints the article on a 3x5 card to concretize the word but does not expect the student to read it.
- Student touches each square and says the sentence.
- Teacher or the student makes a change to the sentence by moving either the noun or the verb.
- Student touches each square and says the sentence.

Once your student becomes accustomed to the initial article, take the little step of staying at a three-word sentence and add the *and* connector between two nouns (even though without a verb you are taking license with an incomplete sentence). In introducing *Cat and dog*, have three colored squares with toys placed on the outside squares, leaving an empty square in the middle for the abstract *and*. You may write the word *and* on a 3x5 card or not, depending on the needs and level of your student. Changing one word at a time, change the sentence to say *Cat and duck*, and then to say *Dog and duck*.

With the abstract *and* established for your student, take the next little step and add a verb (some action) to the end. For example, *dog and duck* can easily change to the complete sentence *Dog and duck jump*. At this point, you determine whether to use a Movement Card for *jump* or to rely on your student's imagery. You are the diagnostician, and you just overlapped to a four-word sentence with four colored squares.

Four- and Seven-Word Sentences

A marker for extending the amount of words in a sentence is the fluency and the imagery you are noting in the student at the three-word level. However, even without complete fluency or evidence of imagery, keep moving your student forward.

For example, you can extend *Cat runs up* to *The cat runs up.* Using the same techniques you've observed with Miss Billie and Chip, add the colored square and write the article on a 3x5 card. You know your student, his age, and his needs. Or you can move from three to four-word sentences with more concreteness, such as *Cat runs up* to *Cat runs up tree.* You can put a picture card on the noun *tree* or you can let your student picture a tree. Again, your choices depend on the needs of your student.

As stated earlier, you can also move from three to four words by extending *Cat and dog* to *Cat and dog jump.* Note how easily you can move your student to a five-word sentence such as *The cat and dog jump.* You can concretize the subject at anytime with a toy or picture card. The possibilities rely on your diagnosis. Plan your strategies based on the gestalt of teaching your student to dual code.

Talking Sentences moves to four-, five-, six,- and seven-word sentences, but not beyond a seven-word sentence, as the level of abstraction becomes too difficult to visualize and recall. Given the abstraction element, as the student moves into the seven-word sentence, he may need to use an object or picture card to concretize the longer, abstract sentence that may now have more articles and connectors.

Rather than extend beyond seven-word sentences, overlap to the next steps of *Talkies.* Continue to do a few Talking Sentences for practice and automaticity, especially working on the rhythm and flow of expressive language, but move on to the next steps of Simple Picture to Picture and Simple Word Imaging. Overlapping allows the continuation of a step while extending the stimulation, but, just as important, overlapping keeps the pace of the stimulation moving and changing—very important for our *Talkies* students.

Sequencing from Two- to Seven-Word Sentences

While the concretizing of language with imagery aids in verbal expression, the exposure needs to occur in small steps to ensure success. Two- to three-word sentences move from the noun and the verb to an adjective, concept, and connector such as:

1) noun + verb = Cat runs.

2) adjective + noun + verb = Yellow cat runs.

3) noun + verb + concept = Cat runs up.

4) article + noun + verb = A cat runs.

5) noun + connector + noun = Cat and dog.

When you move from three- to four-word sentences, the options are many.

> You may change from a three- to a four-word sentence like this,
>
> > Yellow cat runs. *Yellow cat runs up.*
>
> Or you may change from a three- to four-word sentence like this,
>
> > Cat runs up. *Cat runs up tree.*
>
> Or you may change from a three- to four-word sentence like this,
>
> > Cat and dog. *Cat and dog run.*

When you move from four- to seven-word sentences, the options are nearly infinite.

> You may change from a four- to seven-word sentence like this,
>
> > Cat runs up tree. *Cat runs up the tree. A cat runs up the tree. A yellow cat runs up the tree.*

There are many ways to extend sentences, especially when you are in four-, five-, six-, or seven-word sentences. You can add prepositions with a colored square and a written word on a 3x5 card, such as *A cat runs up the tree*, and *A cat runs to the tree.* You are the diagnostician delivering differentiated instruction; therefore, based on your student's response, you may choose to remove the toys or picture cards from the colored squares at the two-word sentence level, or keep them all or partially on the colored squares through the four- to seven-word sentence level. There are sample sentences in the *Talkies* Word and Sentence Reference.

Lesson Summary:
Four- to Seven-Word Sentences

- Build sentences sequentially.
- Do not go beyond a seven-word sentence.
- May concretize a word at any time with an object or a card.

Talking Sentences for Prosody

Prosody is the study of the rhythm of spoken language, including stress and intonation. When the student is doing three-word sentences with the colored squares, playing with the sentence is fun and helpful for developing the rhythm of expressive language. Since the colored square manipulatives represent words in a sentence, they can be moved up and down on the table to play with language.

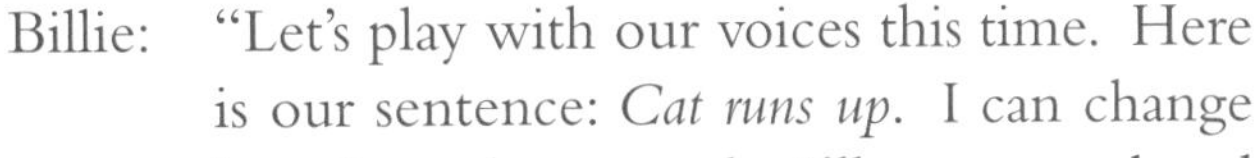

Talking Sentences for Prosody

Billie: "Let's play with our voices this time. Here is our sentence: *Cat runs up*. I can change how I say those words. I'll move a colored square up when I'm going to say a word louder. *CAT runs up*." She moves the first square up and says the word *cat* really loud. "Let's do it together."

Chip: "CAT runs up."

Billie: "Great. Now let's put them back and say this one loud." She puts all the colored squares in a line again, left to right, and then moves the middle square up. "**Cat RUNS up**. Let's do it together."

Chip: "Cat RUNS up."

They practice that a bit longer, and as Miss Billie overlaps steps and feels Chip can comprehend and image better, she explains how emphasizing a word focuses his imagery.

Billie: "When we say a word loud it makes us picture that word the most. Like when I say *Cat RUNS up*, I know the biggest thing I'm going to picture is the cat *running* up, not the cat *jumping* up. But when I say, *CAT runs up*, I know the most important thing in my picture is that a *cat* runs up, not a *dog* runs up."

Lesson Summary:
Talking Sentences for Prosody

- Teacher lines up the colored squares for a simple sentence.
- Teacher moves the first square up and says that word louder.
- Student says the sentence with the emphasized word.
- Teacher moves the first square down, moves the second up, and says the sentence with the new emphasis.
- Student says the sentence with the emphasized word.
- Teacher explains how saying a word loud makes that word's image the most important.

Error Handling

As you practice with your student, you may find that a word is omitted or substituted. The lesson below demonstrates how to handle an error at the two-word level.

Before we begin, here are the principles of error handling: 1) note the student's response, 2) find a spot in his response from which to positively engage him, 3) help the student analyze his response, and 4) help him compare his response to the stimulus. You judge if Miss Billie follows them or not.

SAMPLE LESSON

Talking Two-Word Sentences with Teacher Generating the Change

ERROR: Chip gives an incorrect response when a word is substituted in the sentence.

Billie: "Let's change it again. This one says *Chip jumps*. Let's make it say *Cow jumps*. Which word changed?"

Chip: "Cow jumps." He touches the colored squares as he says the new sentence and then points to the picture of Chip.

Billie: "Right. *Chip* is gone. Take him out and get a new square."

Chip: "Cow. This cow." He picks up the cow and puts it on the new square.

Billie: "Good job! Touch each word and say the sentence for me."

Chip: "Chip jumps."

Billie: "You are right, this is *jump*. You said 'Chip jumps.'" She takes his hand and touches the first square. "Is this *Chip* on this square?"

Chip: "No! Cow."

Billie: "Right! Now touch and say those words."

Chip: "Cow jumps."

Miss Billie has helped Chip compare his response to the stimulus. She can very quickly take it a step further and help him contrast his error with the correct response by saying, "If we want this to say *Chip jumps*, we have to have Chip's picture here." Or she can let him show her: "What do we have to do to make this say *Chip jumps*?"

Concretize and Sequence Language with Imagery

The Talking Sentences step progresses in a sequence to develop imagery and uses that imagery to concretize language expression. Concrete language is more easily processed than abstract language and imagery is a means of making language concrete. Imagery is a sensory-cognitive experience that enables us to concretize a word, a sentence, and a story. Unlike a static picture, well-developed imagery expands and extends the language experience.

We can "see" a dog in our mind's eye when we read or hear about a dog. But unlike a static picture, with well-developed imagery we can picture a yellow labrador digging in the sand. We can extend our imagery-language experience because our imagery is dynamic and we can picture the action of the lab spraying sand all around him. We can add more action and more dogs, or we can substitute our yellow lab with a brown and white cocker spaniel, or we can take the dog away and make it an old man digging in the sand. With our imagery, we can see the blue of the ocean and hear the waves or we can see a child running by while the old man digs.

We integrate imagery with language to help verbal expression—exactly what we are doing with *Talkies*, particularly this Talking Sentences step. We are establishing a sensory-language experience, a dual coding experience, to help children "talk sentences."

Practice and Pacing

As usual, it is time to remind you of the importance of overlapping steps in *Talkies*, and not just the little steps within a big step (a chapter), but also the big steps themselves. For example, in doing two- and three-word sentences in Talking Sentences, you are very likely still doing some little steps in the big step of Talking Words. Continue working a step, or steps, until fairly automatic—then move on and overlap to more steps. Keep extending the stimulation for your student and remember that going back and working a little more on a given step is sometimes necessary and helpful to the gestalt of *Talkies*.

Specifically, as you move into Talking Sentences, you are overlapping with Talking Words, and as you progress to three- and four-word sentences in Talking Sentences, you are likely also overlapping to the next step, Simple Picture to Picture. You may even begin to overlap to Simple Word Imaging—two steps away from where we are now.

Summary: Step 4

Talking Sentences

Goal: To develop imagery and increase the complexity and length of sentences in expressive language.

1. Talking Two-Word Sentences with Teacher Generating the Change

- Teacher creates a sentence with a noun and a verb.
- Language is concretized on colored squares with toys or picture cards.
- Teacher changes one word at a time.
- Teacher starts with a noun on the first square and a Movement Card on the second square.
- Student touches each square and says sentence.
- Teacher changes a word.
- Student touches each square and says the sentence.
- Student changes the square or the square and the card, as appropriate.

2. Talking Two-Word Sentences with Student Generating the Change

- Student chooses an object and a Movement Card and places them on colored squares.
- Student touches each square and says the sentence.

- Student chooses a new object or Movement Card, changing one word in the sentence.
- Student changes the square or the square and card, as appropriate.
- Student touches each square and says the sentence.

3. Talking Two-Word Sentences with Imagery for the Verb

- Teacher creates a two-word sentence without concretizing the verb with a Movement Card.
- Student pictures the verb.
- Teacher changes one word in the sentence.
- Student touches each square and says the sentence.
- Student may act out the verb and may take a turn making the changes in the sentence.
- A colored square changes when a word changes.

4. Talking Two-Word Sentences with Imagery for Whole Sentence

- Teacher creates a sentence without placing objects and cards on the squares.
- Student touches each square and says the sentence.
- Teacher encourages the student to picture.
- Teacher changes one word in the sentence.
- Student touches each square and says the sentence.
- Student may make the change and verbalize the sentence.

5. Adjectives for a Three-Word Sentence

- Teacher places a new square and adds an adjective before the noun in the sentence.
- Student touches each square and says the sentence.
- Teacher encourages the student to picture.
- The words may or may not be concretized on the sentence.

6. Concept Cards for a Three-Word Sentence

- The Concept Cards are used at the end of a sentence.
- Student chooses the Concept Card to put on a square.
- Student touches each square and says the sentence.
- Teacher or the student changes a word in the sentence.

7. Adding Articles and Connectors

- Student says a two-word sentence.
- Teacher places a new square to represent the article.
- Teacher uses the *Talkies* Article Cards or prints the article on a 3x5 card to concretize the word but does not expect the student to read it.
- Student touches each square and says the sentence.
- Teacher or the student makes a change to the sentence by moving either the noun or the verb.
- Student touches each square and says the sentence.

8. Four- to Seven-Word Sentences

- Build sentences sequentially.
- Do not go beyond a seven-word sentence.
- May concretize a word at any time with an object or a card.

9. Talking Sentences for Prosody

- Teacher lines up the colored squares for a simple sentence.
- Teacher moves the first square up and says that word louder.
- Student says the sentence with the emphasized word.
- Teacher moves the first square down, moves the second up, and says the sentence with the new emphasis.
- Student says the sentence with the emphasized word.
- Teacher explains how saying a word loud makes that word's image the most important.

Group Instruction

Modify the Talking Sentences step with the varying skill levels of your students in mind. If there is a wide range in their levels of proficiency, you will need to have each student practice a sentence suitable for them, moving randomly from student to student. If their levels of ability are fairly close, then you can use one master sentence for the entire group, with you and the students both making changes to it. Call on each student randomly to change a single word, and then have the whole group participate by verbalizing the sentence together.

9 Simple Picture to Picture

Simple Picture to Picture is modified from the Picture to Picture step in the *V/V* program. The goal of this step is to develop verbalization from a given picture, using the Picture Structure Words for details to increase the length and complexity of expressive language.

The instruction in the *V/V* Picture to Picture step asks for verbalizing, not visualizing from a student. A visual picture is given to your student from which he will verbalize, giving him practice verbalizing without the added task of trying to create a mental representation to talk from, something he will likely have difficulty doing vividly or quickly.

While *V/V* Picture to Picture is now an old friend to many educators and parents, the step almost didn't exist. Originally, in creating the *V/V* program, I thought we only had to stimulate imagery—I thought we could begin with imagery stimulation. Hence, in the early stages of writing *V/V*, when a student of any age had difficulty verbalizing his or her images, I assumed the weakness was in imagery. But as time passed, it became evident that the problem may not just be the intensity or strength of an individual's imagery. I began to realize that without a window into the student's brain, I didn't know if her trouble was that she couldn't easily visualize or perhaps that she couldn't easily verbalize. I began to ask myself whether the problem was weak imagery, weak expressive language, or both. Was it visualizing or verbalizing? Given that I couldn't be sure where the weakness was, I thought it best to directly develop verbalization. So the *V/V* Picture to Picture step was born, to stimulate verbalizing from a given picture. My thinking was, if I knew the students could describe a given picture, then they could describe their own mental representations. The important instructional step of Picture to Picture, which develops detailed verbalization, emerged from working with students—from practice, not theory.

Now, as *Talkies* has been chipped from the marble of *V/V,* the Picture to Picture step is simplified, with some new little steps added. As before, experience working with students has provided us insight. *Talkies* students need to begin with kinesthetic input; hence the little step of Object to Picture was born.

A Look at Chip Now

As we look in with Miss Billie and Chip, he is beginning his seventh week of *Talkies*. Happier, with growing success in school and at home, he continues to show evidence of dual coding ability. His imagery ability is beginning to improve, though it appears to be slow. His expressive language is also beginning to improve. He talks in more complete sentences, often spontaneously adding an article, a connector, and/or a descriptor. In general, he is moving along. There are fewer behavior issues and he seems able to follow directions better. He regularly makes eye contact, and he is significantly less reclusive. While his social interaction is improved, he still seems to be left out of activities with other children. He is responding, but he is not done. Miss Billie continues to consciously note Chip's responses to instruction, though it appears to him that she simply enjoys their games.

Object to Picture

Rather than beginning with a two-dimensional picture for your student to describe to you as in the *V/V* program, the task is reduced to your student describing a three-dimensional object that he can touch and feel. After his experience with his "magic hands" in the Magic Bag activities, this task is familiar and likely to result in success. As he improves at describing an object, he will be overlapped to describing a picture. In both tasks, he uses structure words for details and he knows his words will create images for you.

Let's visit them now, as Miss Billie uses an object to introduce Chip to "Your words made me picture...." She is overlapping him to the Simple Picture to Picture step now that he is successful at the three-word sentence level in Talking Sentences, and she continues to include Talking Sentences as part of every instructional session with him. She is driving the sensory bus with her language, re-setting the climate frequently. Chip describes one of two toys that Miss Billie can't see because they are behind the *Talkies* Magic Door. As before, the Picture Structure Words help Chip note and verbalize details. He learns that his words create imagery for Miss Billie. She tells him what she pictured and guesses the name of the toy before she looks at it.

As you read the lesson below, remember that Miss Billie has put out the toys for Chip to choose from, therefore she knows which ones Chip may describe. Once he chooses a toy to describe, she does not look at it again until the lesson is complete.

SAMPLE LESSON

Object to Picture

Billie: "Let's play a new game with these toys." She puts the little blue teddy bear and the red car on the table. "Now I'm going to put up this Magic Door." She shows him the Magic Door and puts it up so she can't see the toys anymore. "I can't see the toys now. Can you see them?"

Chip: "Yes. I see toys."

Billie: "Great. Choose a toy to tell me about and hide the other one behind you. Did you hide it?"

Chip: "Yes." He puts the teddy bear behind him. Miss Billie does not look, or at least pretends not to see what he did.

Billie: "Don't tell me the name of the toy." She points over the top of the Magic Door. "I can't see it." She needs to know what toy he is going to describe because she has to ask him questions to help him verbalize. "Your words are going to give me a picture in my mind." She points to her head.

Chip: "It is red." He smiles. Now Miss Billie knows it is the little car and she can ask appropriate questions. She gives him a stone.

Billie: "You can touch the toy. But don't let me see it! Let's use our structure words." She puts out the *movement*, *color*, *number*, and *size* structure words, and touches the *size* card. "Can you tell me what size to picture? That might help me."

Chip: "Little. It is little."

Billie: "Hmmm. Is it a red ball?"

Chip: "No!"

Billie: "Okay. I'm picturing something that is little and red. What about the *movement* structure word? Should I picture something that moves?"

Chip: "Yes."

Billie: "How does it move? Does it have legs? Can it walk? Does it have wings? Does it fly? Does it have wheels? Help me get a better picture in my mind."

Chip: "It have wheels."

Billie: "I can picture wheels. Here is our *number* card. How many wheels should I picture? Count them."

Chip: He counts the wheels, smiling. "Four. It have four wheels."

Billie: "Great. Here is what you told me to picture. A little red toy with four wheels. Those words make me picture a truck or a car. I'll guess a car! If I'm right, open the Magic Door so I can see it. If I'm wrong, don't open the door, and tell me more. Is it a little red car?"

Chip: "Yes. It is little red car." Smiling, he lets her see the toy.

Billie: "Great job. Your words helped me picture that in my mind. You get a lot of stones!"

Lesson Summary:
Object to Picture

- Teacher presents two toys for the student to describe.
- Student chooses one toy he wants to describe, hiding it behind the Magic Door so the teacher can't see it.
- Student sees, feels, and describes the toy, using the structure words for details.
- Teacher questions to increase his verbalization, "Your words make me picture...." "What should I picture for ...?"
- Teacher guesses the toy.
- Student opens the Magic Door if teacher got it right.
- Teacher and the student discuss the parts she didn't picture.

Student and Teacher Describe a Picture

In this little step, the teacher and the student look at a picture and describe it, with the student doing most of the verbalization, if possible. Help your student touch and talk about the gestalt and the parts of the picture. As in all *Talkies* instruction, if you need to, you can begin the stimulation at the receptive level where you point and say a part of the picture and the student gives you thumbs-up or thumbs-down, with a verbal *yes* or *no*. Also, if you need to, give choices to assist your student with word retrieval.

In the lesson below, Chip describes a picture, using the Picture Structure Words to assist himself in including elements of detail. Miss Billie helps him summarize the gestalt and details at the conclusion of the lesson.

SAMPLE LESSON

Student and Teacher Describe a Picture

Billie: "Let's play a game with this picture." She shows him the *Talkies* picture of a little boy holding a red car. "Let's see how much you can tell me about the picture. I'll sometimes take a turn too. Here are your structure words." She puts out the *what*, *color*, *size*, *movement*, and *shape* cards on the table. "Touch the parts of the picture you tell me about."

Chip: "Red car." Smiling, he touches the little red car the boy is holding.

Billie: "Good job. That is a red car. Now tell me about the biggest thing in the picture. Is this a picture of a boy or a girl?"

Chip: "A boy. It is a boy."

Billie: "Right. A boy. Tell me as much as you can. I'll give you a stone for every word you say!"

Chip: "Boy, red car. Shoes."

Billie: "Good job. Let's start at the top and go down. Tell me about his head. What do you see here?" She points to the boy's head in the picture. "Tell me as much as you can, like he has red hair—"

Chip: "This is a boy. He have red hair (touching his head) and..." Miss Billie points to more things on the boy's head. "Eyes...ears... nose."

Billie: "Great! You found lots of things to tell me about his head. Take your finger and go down and tell me everything you can."

Chip: "Shirt. Green shirt. Hands. Red car. Little red car in hand." Miss Billie helps him by directing his finger to more parts of the picture. "Pants. Blue pants. Shoes. Brown shoes."

Billie: "So great. Look at the pile of stones you have! I gave you a stone every time you told me a word. Look at all the words you said!"

Chip: He smiles and touches all his stones.

Billie: "Let's go through your structure words and see if you told me everything. This is *what*. Did you tell me about the biggest thing in the picture? The boy?"

Miss Billie checks through the structure words with Chip. He turns over each card and puts it to "sleep" if he told her about that specific detail. They come to the *shape* card. Since he didn't tell her about a shape in the picture, Miss Billie points to the wheels on the car and helps him discern that the wheels are a round shape.

Billie: "I'll tell you about all of this. It is a little boy with a little red car. You do it. You can even use more words than I did."

Chip: "It is a little boy. He have red hair. He have green shirt. He have little red car."

Lesson Summary:
Student and Teacher Describe a Picture

- Teacher and the student look at a simple picture.
- Teacher directs the description to the gestalt and then the details of the picture.
- Student touches and talks about specific parts, using structure words for details.
- Student may place a Magic Stone on the parts he describes.
- Teacher questions the student to increase his verbalization.
- Student may check through the structure words.
- Teacher and the student may take turns describing parts.
- Teacher helps the student summarize all they saw.

Miss Billie decides to give Chip direct stimulation of imagery. Now that verbalizing has been completed on the above picture and Chip is very familiar with it, she takes the picture away and they talk about what they pictured. While the goal of Simple Picture to Picture is to strengthen verbalization, the opportunity to explicitly develop his imagery can't be missed.

SAMPLE LESSON

Imagery Practice After Picture Description

Billie: "Let's practice our picturing in our mind. I'm going to take the picture away. Tell me what you pictured. Did you picture a boy or a girl? Tell me everything you can."

Chip: "I saw a boy. A little red car."

Lesson Summary:
Imagery Practice After Picture Description

- Teacher and the student look again at the picture they have just described.
- Teacher hides the picture.
- Student describes his imagery.
- Teacher questions to direct his imagery, "What did you picture for...?"
- When the student has completed his verbalization, he sees the picture again.
- Teacher looks for signs the student is imaging.
- Teacher may take a turn and tell the student what she remembers to prompt his imagery.

Miss Billie questions Chip for a little bit, stimulating his imagery. She carefully watches him to determine if he is visualizing. She also notes how complete his sentences are, delighted that he is spontaneously beginning to verbalize with more detail, articles, and pronouns.

Simple Picture to Picture

The Simple Picture to Picture step has a student describe a given picture, but now the teacher doesn't look at the picture. The student's words have to create an image for her. This is *V/V* Picture to Picture, only with a very simple picture.

The teacher gives the student a picture and doesn't look at it after giving it to him. He describes the picture and you drive the sensory bus by saying, "Your words make me picture...."

Since you are not able to see the picture, the student knows he really does have to tell you as much as possible; he must verbalize. The structure words are used to assist with detailed verbalization. You have seen the picture prior to giving it to the student to describe, hence you can ask specific questions to develop and extend his verbalization, such as "What should I picture for the color of his hair?"

Remember, you want to say, "What should I picture?" rather than, "What are you picturing?" The goal of the lesson is to develop verbalization, not visualization.

You must carefully choose your language to stimulate the appropriate sensory information.

In the lesson below, Miss Billie gives Chip the *Talkies* picture of a little black-haired girl dressed in a blue dress, running on green grass. She adds a new Picture Structure Word, *where*.

SAMPLE LESSON

Simple Picture to Picture

Billie: "This time you get to see the picture. But I don't! Your words will have to make a picture in my mind. Here is a picture. I'll put the Magic Door in front of it so I can't see it. Tell me everything you can about the picture."

Chip: "It is a girl. She runs."

Billie: "Great. Your words make me picture a girl running. Should I picture a little girl or a big girl?"

Chip: "Little girl."

Billie: "Little like a baby, or little like your size?"

Chip: "Like me."

Billie: "Okay. Your words make me picture a little girl. I picture her about as big as you. Help me picture more about the little girl. Start at the top and go down. What should I picture for her hair?" Miss Billie is drawing on the previous little step of having him touch and describe the picture from the top down.

Chip: "She have black hair."

Miss Billie continues to question with choice and contrast, always using language that refers back to the fact that his words make her create a mental picture. "Your words make me picture...." "That makes me picture...." "Now you're helping me picture...."

When she feels Chip has told her most of the gestalt and details of the picture, they check through the structure words to see if he told her about each of them.

Billie: "Let's check through our structure words and see if we got everything. This time, you touch the card and tell me if you got it. Touch this *what* card. Did you tell me *what*?"

Chip: "Girl. I said girl."

Billie: "Right! Turn the card over and put it to sleep. Keep going, check through each of them."

Chip touches each structure word and uses them to give her detail. If he comes to a structure word he hasn't told her about, he looks at the picture and tells her now. This completed, Miss Billie is ready for a summary.

Billie: "You did so good. I'll tell you what I have pictured. Look at your picture and see if I get everything."

Chip: "Okay."

Billie: "Your words made me picture a little girl with black hair, and she had a blue dress on. She was running on the green grass...." She continues with a full description.

Billie: "Your words really gave me a good picture. How did I do? Did I get it all?"

Chip: "Yes. You got all!"

Billie: "Now open the Magic Door and let me see the picture."

Lesson Summary:
Simple Picture to Picture

- Student hides a picture behind the Magic Door.
- Student describes the picture, using the structure words for detail.
- Teacher questions to increase his verbalization, "Your words make me picture...." "What should I picture for...?"
- Teacher gives a summary after the student has completed his description, "Your words made me picture...."
- Student opens the Magic Door and teacher sees the picture.
- Teacher and the student compare her imagery to the picture.
- Teacher says, "Great, I pictured a...." "I didn't picture this...."

They look at the picture together and she discusses with him that she didn't picture the little girl's red shoes. Pointing to the shoes, she says, "I didn't picture her shoes!" It is important that she own the error rather than blaming him by saying, "You didn't tell me about the shoes."

Choose a Simple Picture

The pictures to describe in *Talkies* are simple with very few details, using basic concepts or words. You do not want the Simple Picture to Picture step to become a vocabulary lesson. Use the following criteria to choose your pictures or use the pictures in the *Talkies* Kit.

- One central figure
- Very little detail on the central figure
- No background details
- Illustrates known vocabulary

Error Handling

Though Chip knows the difference between big and little, in describing a picture with Miss Billie, he points to the little thing in a picture rather than the big thing. She follows the principles of error handling and helps him compare his response to the stimulus.

SAMPLE LESSON

Student and Teacher Describe a Picture

ERROR: Chip gives the wrong choice for the structure word, *size*.

Billie: "Good. Now let's do this structure word." She touches the *size* card. "Point to the big thing in the picture. Find the biggest thing." The boy is the biggest thing in the picture and he is holding a little red car.

Chip: He points to the little car, something he really likes. "Car."

Billie: "You are right, there is a car in the picture. Is the car big or little?"

Chip: "Little."

Billie: "Right. We need to find the big thing in the picture. Let's see if that is the biggest thing. Here are two things." She puts a little square and a big square on the table. "Touch the big square."

Chip: "This big." He knows *big* and *little*, but wasn't attending to her first question. He easily touches the big square. "This big." He touches the boy in the picture and self-corrects. "Boy is big. Car is little."

Miss Billie was certain Chip knew big from little, but that was irrelevant. She always responds to his response and helps him compare his response to the stimulus. She knows that these lessons are about more than just getting an answer right, they are about helping Chip learn to learn.

Practice and Pacing

As you read *Talkies*, you are an observer of the lesson interaction. The sample lessons give you the opportunity to hear and see the necessary interaction of Socratic questioning to directly stimulate the student's sensory system. You are able to visualize not only what the teacher says, but also how she says it, and how she responds to her student with positive energy and immediate rewards. Along with that, you are learning the parts and the whole, to build your own internal schemata from which to pace your student.

Chip may not be stable at Simple Picture to Picture before he is overlapped to Simple Word Imagery, the next step of *Talkies*. Do not continue until there is mastery of a step, instead continue to overlap steps to keep the energy high.

Specifically, as you move into Simple Word Imagery, you may be overlapping with vocabulary work in Talking Words, talking four- and five-word sentences, and Picture to Picture. Your student is using a task chart to know what he has accomplished and how much more he has to go. He relies on the visual representation of his progress to help him see the parts within the whole.

Summary: Step 5

Simple Picture to Picture

Goal: To develop verbalization from a given picture, using the Picture Structure Words for details to increase the length and complexity of expressive language.

1. Object to Picture

- Teacher presents two toys for the student to describe.
- Student chooses one toy he wants to describe, hiding it behind the Magic Door so the teacher can't see it.
- Student sees, feels, and describes the toy, using the structure words for details.
- Teacher questions to increase his verbalization, "Your words make me picture...." "What should I picture for ...?"
- Teacher guesses the toy.
- Student opens the Magic Door if teacher got it right.
- Teacher and the student discuss the parts she didn't picture.

2. Student and Teacher Describe a Picture

- Teacher and the student look at a simple picture.
- Teacher directs the description to the gestalt and then the details of the picture.
- Student touches and talks about specific parts, using structure words for details.

- Student may place a Magic Stone on the parts he describes.
- Teacher questions the student to increase his verbalization.
- Student may check through the structure words.
- Teacher and the student may take turns describing parts.
- Teacher helps the student summarize all they saw.

3. Imagery Practice After Picture Description

- Teacher and the student look again at the picture they have just described.
- Teacher hides the picture.
- Student describes his imagery.
- Teacher questions to direct his imagery, "What did you picture for...?"
- When the student has completed his verbalization, he sees the picture again.
- Teacher looks for signs the student is imaging.
- Teacher may take a turn and tell the student what she remembers to prompt his imagery.

4. Simple Picture to Picture

- Student hides a picture behind the Magic Door.
- Student describes the picture, using the structure words for detail.
- Teacher questions to increase his verbalization, "Your words make me picture...." "What should I picture for...?"
- Teacher gives a summary after the student has completed his description, "Your words made me picture...."
- Student opens the Magic Door and teacher sees the picture.
- Teacher and the student compare her imagery to the picture.
- Teacher says, "Great, I picture a...." "I didn't picture this...."

Group Instruction

The Simple Picture to Picture lessons are easily modified to accommodate the involvement of an entire group. In the Object to Picture little step and the Student and Teacher Describe a Picture little step, have the entire group look at the object/ picture and then question random students to check their imagery, using the structure words to increase the detail of their descriptions. The entire group can build an image together in the Imagery Practice little step, and in the final Simple Picture to Picture step, the whole group can participate in describing the picture to the instructor. Remember to call on students randomly, ensuring that the entire group stays engaged and attentive.

10 Simple Word Imaging

As we move into these latter steps of *Talkies*, the student begins to extend into the first steps of *V/V*, but at a simpler level. The *V/V* Word Imagery step has been chipped into little steps, becoming Simple Word Imaging that directly stimulates the student's ability to create a mental representation from the basic unit of language—a word.

A Look at Chip Now

As we look in with Miss Billie and Chip, he is beginning his ninth week of *Talkies*. He continues to talk in more complete sentences with articles, conjunctions, and prepositions. He is using appropriate verb tenses and pronouns. He now often says, "I'm running" instead of "I run." Miss Billie is excited. The stimulation is working. He is happier, his behavior is improving, and he demonstrates more evidence of dual coding every week.

Yesterday, his father dropped him off. He and Chip came into the room, holding hands. Then Chip let go and went over to be with some other children. Standing and watching Chip laugh and shyly talk with some friends, he turned to Miss Billie and quietly said, "Thank you."

Word to Object to Imagery

Begin word imaging from an object that the student can touch and feel. You say a word and the student finds the toy that represents the word. Then hide the toy and have your student give a verbal description to you. While similar to object imagery as in earlier steps, this stimulation starts with a word and then goes to an object to assist with the imagery of the word.

Choose words and toys that have been experienced by your student throughout *Talkies*. A simple toy such as a ball is a good choice for a severe student, but as the student progresses, extend the stimulation to a more detailed object such as a truck. Consider that your student's images may not be as vivid as yours. Instead, his images may be dim and may fade easily, making them difficult for him to describe. As you question and the student uses the structure words, his mental representations will return and strengthen. Question him to help him create imagery from language. Never assume imagery, instead question him to be sure he is picturing rather than paraphrasing or parroting back one of your choices.

SAMPLE LESSON

Word to Object to Imagery

Billie: She redraws the head and thought bubble. "I'm going to say a word. You picture it. Then you find a toy that matches your picture. The word is *ball*. Picture a ball. Got it?"

Chip: "Yes."

Billie: "Great. Now let's find the toy you pictured." She gets the ball from the *Talkies* Kit. "Take a good look at it. Now I'm going to hide it and you tell me what you picture for the word *ball*." She hides the ball behind her. "What do you picture when I say the word *ball*?"

Chip: "A ball."

Billie: "Right. Tell me as much as you can about what you're picturing for the ball. Use your structure words to help you." She puts out the Picture Structure Words of *what*, *color*, *size*, *where*, *movement*, and *shape*. "What shape are you picturing?"

Chip: "Round."

Billie: "Good. Keep going through the structure words. Touch each one and picture that one for your ball. What about color? What about size? Go!"

Chip: "Round. Red. It is red. Small. It is small."

Billie: "Great. You are picturing a small red ball. And it is round. Keep going. Great picturing. Can you picture the ball moving? Is it bouncing like this, up and down?" She pantomimes a ball bouncing up and down. "Or is it rolling along like this?" She pantomimes rolling. By giving him choices to visualize, Miss Billie tries to extend his imaging ability beyond his recall of the ball on their table.

Chip: "Bouncing."

Billie: "Great! Show me what bouncing would look like."

Chip: Moving his hand up and down, he shows her something that might resemble bouncing.

Billie: "Right! Up and down on the ground. Where do you picture the ball bouncing? Is it bouncing inside the room or outside in the yard?"

Chip: "Outside. It is outside."

Billie: "Great. Where is it outside? Are you picturing it under a tree or in the grass?"

Miss Billie continues to give him choices to keep his imagery active and extending. She is developing his imagery with her questions. If he could visualize easily he wouldn't be a *Talkies* student! Chip needs Miss Billie to ask explicit questions that stimulate his ability to create vivid, active mental representations. After she feels he has completed his verbal description, they go back through the structure words, putting them to "sleep," and he reverbalizes what he told her.

Billie: "Let's check through our structure words and see if you told me everything. Touch each one and put it to sleep if you told it to me." She directs his hand to the *what* structure word. "Did you tell me what you were picturing?"

Chip: "Yes."

Billie: "Did you picture an elephant or a ball?"

Chip: "A ball." He grins. "A red ball."

Billie: "Super. Turn over the *what* card and turn over the *color* card. Keep going. Touch the other cards. Did you tell me this one?" She takes his hand and they touch the *size* card.

Chip: "Little ball." He turns over the *size* card.

Chip: "Round. Round ball." He turns over the *shape* card.

They keep going through the structure words, getting more imagery and verbalization out of the little lesson with the ball. When he finishes putting the structure words to "sleep," she tells him what his words made her picture.

Billie: "Your words made me a picture a little red ball. It was bouncing outside...."

Lesson Summary:
Word to Object to Imagery

- Teacher says a word and asks the student to picture the word and then find a toy to match the word.
- Student finds the toy, touching and feeling it to enhance his imagery.
- Teacher hides the toy and asks the student to picture it and tell her about it.
- Student verbalizes his imagery, using the structure words to aid in details.
- Teacher questions to extend the student's imagery.
- When the student's verbal description is complete, he may check through each structure word again, putting them to "sleep."
- Teacher gives a summary, "Your words made me picture...."
- Teacher and the student look at the toy again to check their imagery.
- The Magic Door can be used to hide the toy.

Word to Picture to Imagery

Word to Picture to Imagery is another little step within the big step of Word Imaging. Instead of having the student see and touch an object, have him look at a picture card to stimulate his imagery of a word.

Similar to the lesson above, Miss Billie gives Chip a word, then he finds a picture of the word. The structure words help him visualize and verbalize.

SAMPLE LESSON

Word to Picture to Imagery

Billie: She redraws the head and thought bubble. "I'm going to say a word. You picture it. Then you find a picture card that matches your picture. The word is *cow*. Picture a cow. Got it?"

Chip: "Yes. A cow."

Billie: "Great. Find the picture card of a cow. Take a good look at it."

Chip: He finds the cow picture card and studies it.

Billie: "Now I'm going to hide the picture and you tell me what you picture for the word *cow*" She hides the cow behind the Magic Door. "What do you picture when I say the word *cow*?"

Chip: "A cow."

Billie: "Right. Tell me as much as you can about what you're picturing for the cow. Use your structure words to help you." She puts out the Picture Structure Words. "What color are you picturing?"

Chip: "Black."

Billie: "Good. Your words make me picture a cow that is all black. Is it all black or is there also some white?"

Chip: "Black and white. The cow is black and white."

Billie: "Great! Your words are making me picture a black and white cow. Keep going. Use your structure words if you want to."

Miss Billie and Chip continue through the lesson

with her questioning him to stimulate and extend his imagery. When he seems to have completed his imagery, he checks through the structure words one more time, and puts them to "sleep" as he reverbalizes his imagery.

Billie: "Great job, Chip. Every structure word is asleep now. Let me tell you what your words made me picture. I saw a black and white cow, standing in green grass...."

When Miss Billie finishes describing her imagery, she and Chip open the Magic Door and compare their imagery to the picture.

Lesson Summary:
Word to Picture to Imagery

- Teacher says a word and asks the student to picture the word and then find a picture card to match the word.
- Student finds the card and looks at it carefully before the teacher hides it behind the Magic Door.
- Student verbalizes his imagery, using the structure words to aid in details.
- Teacher questions to extend student's imagery.
- When the student's verbal description is complete, he may check through each structure word again, putting them to "sleep."
- Teacher gives a summary, "Your words made me picture...."
- Teacher and the student open the Magic Door and compare their imagery to the picture card.

Known Noun Imaging

As soon as the student has experienced some success visualizing a word that was connected to a recalled image, overlap him to creating a mental representation from a known noun. A known noun is a word that the student is familiar with and perhaps has experienced—and the word should be high in imagery. For example, *tree* is a word that is familiar, but not necessarily high in imagery. *Christmas tree* is also likely to be familiar but it is high in imagery. Given that the goal is to stimulate the student's imagery, it is important to choose nouns high in imagery. Samples of such high-imagery nouns are included in the *Talkies* Word and Sentence Reference. However, if a noun isn't high in imagery, you can question to extend the imagery around the noun. For example, a cat is familiar and not necessarily high in imagery, but you can ask questions that will bring more imagery into the lesson. You might help the student create more vivid images by having the cat move (the *movement* structure word). You might help him create more vivid images by having him place the cat somewhere with high imagery (the *where* structure word). If you do this, remember to keep your questions primarily focused on the cat doing something or being somewhere, rather than leading your student off into a new direction.

You know your student's oral vocabulary level by this time and you will use known nouns and questions appropriate to his level. Here is a sample of known nouns: dog, cat, tiger, cow, fish, ball, balloon, clown, doll, boat, pig, airplane, truck, elephant, and birthday cake. Do not have your student visualize and describe a person. Although they are familiar, they are too difficult to describe.

To make this task a little easier than Word Imaging in *V/V*, the teacher takes a turn adding to Chip's imagery. This is similar to when you work with groups of students where each student adds something to the image. In this case, Chip is picturing from Miss Billie's questions, but he is also going to add an element from her specific imagery.

Let's look in on Miss Billie and Chip. She is overlapping from a lesson where she said a word and then Chip saw a picture of the word prior to visualizing it. Now she just says a word and has Chip visualize it.

SAMPLE LESSON

Known Noun Imaging

Billie: "I'm going to say a word and you tell me what you picture. *Dog*. What does that word make you picture?"

Chip: "A dog."

Billie: "Yes, a dog. Let's go through your structure words. What color is your dog?" She touches the *color* structure word. "And what size is your dog? Your words are going to give me a picture in my head, too. What color do you picture your dog? Is he brown or yellow or...."

Chip: "Dog is white."

Billie: "White! Great. I can make my dog white, too. Keep going through the structure words."

Chip: "Dog is little." He touches the *size* card.

Chip: "Dog is running." He touches the *movement* card.

Billie: "Great. Let me take a turn." She touches the *where* card. "I picture a little white dog and he is running in the grass. Can you picture that?"

Chip: "Yes."

Billie: "Great. What does it look like? What color is the grass?"

Chip: "I see grass. The grass is green. He is running in grass."

Billie: "Great. How is he running? Really fast or sort of slow?"

Chip: "He is running fast."

Miss Billie continues to help Chip get a vivid picture of the word, but she doesn't overdo the lesson. She watches him closely to see if he is picturing—and also if he is fatiguing. She knows the lesson directly challenges his weakness. She must push him just enough, but not too much.

She thinks Chip has had enough questioning and imagery stimulation, so she has him check through

the structure words and put them to "sleep."

Billie: "Great job. Let's take turns going through the structure words and see if we got everything. My turn first." She touches the *what* card. "We pictured a dog. Put that one to sleep. Now your turn."

Chip: "He was little dog." He turns over the *what* and the *size* cards.

Miss Billie quickly completes that task and moves to describing her picture.

Billie: "Your words made me picture...."

Lesson Summary:
Known Noun Imaging

- Teacher says a known noun and asks the student to picture it.
- Student verbalizes his imagery, using the structure words to aid in details.
- Teacher questions to extend the student's imagery.
- Teacher looks for signs that student is imaging.
- Teacher may take a turn visualizing.
- When the student's verbal description is complete, he may check through each structure word again, putting them to "sleep."
- Teacher gives a summary, "Your words made me picture...."

Practice and Pacing

You are now familiar with overlapping steps, so you know to drop some steps and to extend others. The step you want to continue throughout *Talkies* is the development of oral vocabulary. With your student progressing to Simple Word Imaging, you are starting to be comfortable with his imaging ability and you have noticed improvement in his expressive language. But you do not want to stop extending his oral vocabulary so you continue to note words he has difficulty with, putting those words on cards or lists for reinforcement.

Summary: Step 6

Simple Word Imaging

Goal: The goal of this step is to develop visualization from the smallest unit of language—a word.

1. Word to Object to Imagery

- Teacher says a word and asks the student to picture the word and then find a toy to match the word.
- Student finds the toy, touching and feeling it to enhance his imagery.
- Teacher hides the toy and asks the student to picture it and tell her about it.
- Student verbalizes his imagery, using the structure words to aid in details.
- Teacher questions to extend the student's imagery.
- When the student's verbal description is complete, he may check through each structure word again, putting them to "sleep."
- Teacher gives a summary, "Your words made me picture...."
- Teacher and the student look at the toy again to check their imagery.
- The Magic Door can be used to hide the toy.

2. Word to Picture to Imagery

- Teacher says a word and asks the student to picture the word and then find a picture card to match the word.
- Student finds the card and looks at it carefully before the teacher hides it behind the Magic Door.
- Student verbalizes his imagery, using the structure words to aid in details.
- Teacher questions to extend the student's imagery.
- When the student's verbal description is complete, he may check through each structure word again, putting them to "sleep."
- Teacher gives a summary, "Your words made me picture…."
- Teacher and the student open the Magic Door and compare their imagery to the picture card.

3. Known Noun Imaging

- Teacher says a known noun and asks the student to picture it.
- Student verbalizes his imagery, using the structure words to aid in details.
- Teacher questions to extend the student's imagery.
- Teacher looks for signs that student is imaging.
- Teacher may take a turn visualizing.
- When the student's verbal description is complete, he may check through each structure word again, putting them to "sleep."
- Teacher gives a summary, "Your words made me picture…."

Group Instruction

In the Word to Object to Imagery and the Word to Picture to Imagery lessons, have the students take turns finding the items you describe. For the remainder of those lessons, and in the Known Noun Imaging lesson as well, call randomly on students in the group to give descriptions. Encourage students to respond nonverbally to the responses of their peers, with thumbs-up or thumbs-down gestures.

11 Simple Sentence Imaging

Chip is now about to visualize and verbalize a simple sentence. *Talkies,* like *V/V,* moves from the Known Noun step to the Simple Sentence step, using a known noun that has just been imaged to concretize the subject of a sentence. While the smallest unit of language after a word is a phrase, however phrases can be more abstract to visualize than a sentence.

The goal of Simple Sentence Imaging is to develop visualizing and verbalizing for a sentence. Simple. The instructional procedures are the same as in word imaging and are very familiar to the student. Much like what you can expect your student to do at this stage of *Talkies*, Chip is beginning to consciously connect imagery to language. He still plays with numerous words in sentences in Talking Sentences, he makes his voice go louder as he moves colored squares up and down in a sentence, he describes pictures in Simple Picture and Picture, he visualizes known nouns, and he practices his own vocabulary words.

Chip's affect is also improving. It is week ten, Chip makes eye contact, smiles, and attends fairly well in his classroom. Despite good progress in the last ten weeks, he is still not done. His imaging doesn't appear fast and vivid. Miss Billie still heavily questions him to stimulate imagery. However, the more she sees him respond and move through the steps of *Talkies*, the more encouraged she is that she's driving the right bus.

Visualizing and Verbalizing a Simple Sentence

Having reached this step in *Talkies,* there is very little new for you to learn instructionally in order to teach your student to visualize and verbalize a simple sentence. You will use the same instructional sequence of Socratic interaction, responding to his response, giving immediate rewards, and using structure words to assist with detailed imagery. The interaction and steps are familiar to both you and your student, making it easy to overlap from imaging a word to imaging a simple sentence.

At the Simple Sentence level you build parts to a whole, words to a sentence. Students visualize the sentence and then verbalize their imagery. While the step is easy, you need to (1) choose words and concepts in the sentence that the student has experienced with you, and (2) use high-imagery sentences that may incorporate sound effects. The use of a sound effect can enhance imagery and possibly make the imagery more vivid. Samples of high-imagery sentences are provided in the *Talkies* Word and Sentence Reference.

As we look in on Miss Billie and Chip, he has just completed imaging *dog* as his known noun. Miss Billie is overlapping to Simple Sentence Imaging while she continues to strengthen his word imaging. She is now holding hands with a lot of the *Talkies* steps. As she moves into Simple Sentence Imaging, she is considering taking a turn to help him visualize, just as she sometimes did with word imaging. However, she's going to see how the lesson goes and if he does well, she'll let him go without input of her imagery. She knows she can give him help with imagery any time he needs it.

Visualizing and Verbalizing a Simple Sentence

Billie: "Now that we have such a good picture for your dog, let's picture him doing something new. Here it is: *The dog barked at the mouse.* What do those words make you picture?"

Chip: "Dog barked at mouse."

Billie: "Right. The dog barked at the mouse. Can you still see the dog that you just pictured? Tell me about him really quickly."

Chip: "The dog is big. He is yellow. He has long tail. He has big eyes. He has legs. Four legs. He runs fast."

Billie: "Right. Now change your picture to match *The dog barks at the mouse.* What do you see your dog doing now?"

Chip: "He is barking. He barking at the mouse."

Billie: "Good. He is barking at the mouse. What does it look like when the dog is barking? Can you picture his mouth open or his mouth closed?"

Chip: "Mouth open."

Billie: "Yes. His mouth would have to be open. Show me your mouth open."

Chip: He opens his mouth, then smiles.

Billie: "Right. We can picture the dog's mouth open. The sentence said *The dog barks at the mouse.* What does a bark sound like? Let's make one." She thinks that if Chip can't make a barking sound, she'll prompt it, but she is going to try to get him to do it first.

Chip: "Woof. Woof. Woof." He smiles.

Billie: "Great! You have a great bark! Now we can picture the dog barking. What do we picture him barking at? The sentence was *The dog barks at the mouse.* What do you picture for the mouse?"

Chip: "A little mouse. This little." He shows a little mouse with his hands, something he and Miss Billie had been doing a lot of over the last few weeks—gesturing his imagery.

Miss Billie continues to question Chip for more details in his imagery and more verbalization, and then she has him check through the Picture Structure Words, which have been face down in front of him.

Billie: "Your words made me have a good picture of the yellow dog barking at the little gray mouse. Now let's check through the structure words. They are all asleep right here." She puts them out, turned over, the *what* card first. "Wake them up and let's make sure we got them in our picture. Start with this one." She points to the *what* card.

Chip: "A dog. A big yellow dog. He barking at a mouse."

Billie: "Right! That card is awake. Do the next one."

They "wake up" each structure word, she questions him to ensure he reverbalizes all the detail. Miss Billie gives Chip a summary.

Billie: "You be the teacher, Chip. See if I'm right. Your words made me picture a big yellow dog barking at a little mouse with little eyes and a long tail. He was a little gray mouse...."

Lesson Summary:
Visualizing and Verbalizing a Simple Sentence

- Teacher creates a simple sentence using the known noun just visualized and verbalized in the Word Imaging step.
- Teacher questions with choice and contrast to help the student develop detailed, vivid imagery and verbalization.
- Student checks through the structure words after he has visualized and verbalized the sentence.
- He "wakes up" the structure words and reverbalizes his imagery.
- Teacher summarizes, "Your words made me picture...."
- Student may keep the structure words in front of him to assist his imaging.
- Use sound effects to assist in developing vivid imagery.

Visualizing and Verbalizing a Phrase

As noted earlier, without a subject a phrase is more abstract to visualize than a simple sentence. However, you may have a student that you believe can benefit from specifically visualizing and verbalizing a phrase. Not only is the instructional sequence similar to word and sentence imaging, but the student has also already encountered the basic concepts of a phrase when he used the Concept Cards in the Talking Sentences step. Those cards are now used as a little step for visualizing and verbalizing a phrase.

SAMPLE LESSON

Using a Concept Card to Visualize and Verbalize a Phrase

Billie: This time we'll picture concepts, like on your Concept Cards." She gets out the familiar Concept Cards he used in the Talking Sentences step and puts four cards on the floor where they are working. "I'll say a word and you point to the card: *up*."

Chip: "This one." He points to the *up* card.

Billie: "Right. It is that one. Picture your hand going up. Show me your hand going up."

Chip: Closing his eyes briefly, he moves his hand up.

Billie: "Right again. That is up. Now tell me what you do, like this, *My hand goes up*." She makes her hand go up. "You say that and do it."

Chip: "My hand goes up." He moves his hand up.

Billie: "Great. It is my turn to point. It is your turn to talk. What is this card?" She points to the *down* card.

Chip: "Down. It down. It is down." He smiles and seems proud of himself for saying a longer sentence, something they are working on in the Talking Sentences step.

Billie: "Good talking, Chip! It is down! Picture your hand going down. Now show me your hand going down."

Chip: "Down." He moves his hand down. "My hand is down."

Lesson Summary:
Using a Concept Card to Visualize and Verbalize a Phrase

- Teacher says a concept.
- Student finds the Concept Card.
- Teacher says an action involving the concept.
- Student performs the action and verbalizes it.

They practice a little bit more and then take the cards away to begin visualizing and verbalizing a phrase without visual assistance from a card.

SAMPLE LESSON

Visualizing and Verbalizing a Phrase

Billie: "Let's put the cards away and you just use your picturing." She shows him the head and the thought bubble again. "Here we go. Picture this: *Up an arm.* Show me this little car going up an arm."

Chip: "Up arm." He moves the car up Miss Billie's arm.

Billie: "Great. This time picture your hand *on the table.* What do those words make you picture?"

Chip: "Hand on table. My hand on the table."

Billie: "Right! Show me what it looks like to put your hand on the table."

Chip: He puts his hand on the table.

Billie: "Good job. Now picture your hand *under the table*." She pauses to give him time to image. "Show me what you pictured. Put your hand under the table."

Chip: He puts his hand under the table.

Billie: "Great. Now tell me what you did."

Chip: "My hand under the table."

Lesson Summary:
Visualizing and Verbalizing a Phrase

- Teacher says a phrase.
- Student pictures the phrase, then does the action and verbalizes it.

Visualize and verbalize phrases that are difficult for your student, using not only the student's body but also an object such as a toy. You can begin nearly any stimulation at the receptive level, hence you could picture, say, and do a concept and merely have your student judge right or wrong. Remember, the principle behind receptive practice is that if the student can monitor your words or actions, then he is able to monitor his own words or actions.

Error Handling

In Simple Sentence Imaging, Chip has difficulty either in holding his image or in describing what he visualizes. In either case, without a window into his brain, Miss Billie can only respond to his response and use the four principles of error handling to close the circle for Chip.

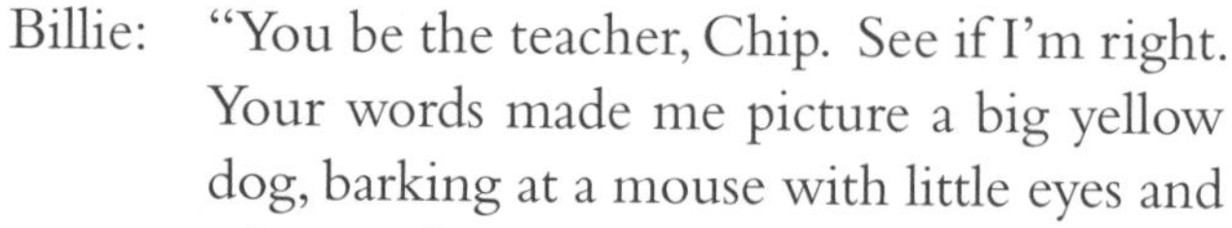

Visualizing and Verbalizing a Simple Sentence

ERROR: Chip changes a detail in the sentence during the summary.

Billie: "You be the teacher, Chip. See if I'm right. Your words made me picture a big yellow dog, barking at a mouse with little eyes and a long tail. He was a little gray mouse."

Chip: "No, big mouse!"

Billie: "When you say *big mouse*, are you picturing him big like an elephant? Big like a horse? Big like the dog?"

Chip: He smiles. "He not big. He is little. He is a little mouse."

Billie: "Right. If you say big mouse, then those words made me picture that the mouse was big like this." She holds her arms above her head to exaggerate the image. "Wow! That would be a big mouse."

Practice and Pacing

Talkies students, like *V/V* students, often repeat the stimulus words rather than create vivid imagery. It is important to remind you again not to assume imagery, especially with our *Talkies* students. Even if a student repeats the same words to you and it seems he is imaging, do not assume he is imaging. Instead, ask questions to verify his imagery and increase its vividness and detail.

As in all *Talkies* steps, it is important to practice to increase the speed of imagery and then overlap to the next step to extend the imagery and verbalization. You are about to start the Sentence by Sentence step of *Talkies*, the heart of *V/V*. The prerequisite to visualizing and verbalizing multiple sentences is strong imagery for a single sentence. Practice this step until you notice less questioning is needed from you to elicit your student's imagery and verbalization.

Summary: Step 7

Simple Sentence Imaging

Goal: The goal of this step is to develop visualizing and verbalizing for a single sentence.

1. Visualizing and Verbalizing a Simple Sentence

- Teacher creates a simple sentence using the known noun just visualized and verbalized in the Word Imaging step.
- Teacher questions with choice and contrast to help the student develop detailed, vivid imagery and verbalization.
- Student checks through the structure words after he has visualized and verbalized the sentence.
- He "wakes up" the structure words and reverbalizes his imagery.
- Teacher summarizes, "Your words made me picture...."
- Student may keep the structure words in front of him to assist his imaging.
- Use sound effects to assist in developing vivid imagery.

2. Using a Concept Card to Visualize and Verbalize a Phrase

- Teacher says a concept.
- Student finds the Concept Card.

- Teacher says an action involving the concept.
- Student performs the action and verbalizes it.

3. Visualizing and Verbalizing a Phrase

- Teacher says a phrase.
- Student pictures the phrase, then does the action and verbalizes it.

Group Instruction

The Simple Sentence Imaging lessons are done with a group of students in the same manner as they are with a single student. Read the sentence to the entire group and then, using the structure words to build detailed imagery, question random students on each structure word. Be sure to include and encourage gesturing in the lesson, as it helps all students in the group build the same image.

12 Talking Picture Stories

The goal of Talking Picture Stories is to directly develop imagery and expressive language by sequencing a series of pictures into a little story, parts to whole. The pictures are described, ordered, visualized, and then reverbalized from imagery. The student verbalizes a picture story first from the given pictures *and then from his own imagery.*

Chip is about to begin this step as an expressive six year old. Instead of sad eyes and a loud frustrated voice saying over and over, "Duck park, duck park," he now says, "I want to go to the park. I want to feed the ducks."

He regularly uses articles, connectors, pronouns, and prepositions. His vocabulary is expanding. He makes eye contact and demonstrates a self-confidence that was lacking a few months ago. He is usually interactive rather than withdrawn in social settings. He doesn't appear as shy or as separate; instead, he usually understands others and expresses himself with language. His family indicates he appears happier and includes himself more in the family. His teacher wrote she thinks he is maturing because he socializes more with other students. However, more than likely what appears to be "maturation" is really his improved communication skills, which enable him to participate and interact with adults and peers, and also control his behavior. The latter is important because his occasional poor behavior may have been attributed to immaturity rather than weakness in his sensory processing.

While Chip continues to move successfully through *Talkies* and has made good progress, Miss Billie knows he needs continued direct stimulation because his dual coding does not appear to be rapid and automatic. There is a delay in his imagery and verbalization, a slowness that might be expected after a relatively short period of stimulation. Her fear is that unless direct stimulation is continued, he may plateau and experience significant difficulty in the ensuing grades.

Sequencing Picture Stories

With the *Talkies* Picture Sequence Cards, picture sequencing begins at the lowest level possible, two pictures, and then extends to three, four, and five pictures. To sequence picture cards the student must grasp the concepts of *first* and *last*, something your student learned in previous lessons with the Concept Cards. And though you may be fairly confident that your student knows *first* and *last*, check for mastery by doing simple tasks such as placing three colored squares on the table and asking him to touch the first square and the last square.

The approach is familiar to you now. Use Socratic questioning to develop your student's imagery and verbal expression. Show him pictures, question to help him describe each picture and note specific details to help determine the sequence, and then have him touch and tell a story from the cards.

The *Talkies* Picture Sequence Cards illustrate fun and familiar activities and are in color to reduce figure-ground problems for the student.

Lesson Summary:
Sequencing Picture Stories

- Teacher checks to be sure the student has mastery of the concepts *first* and *last*.
- Teacher places Picture Sequence Cards in random order for the student to describe.
- Teacher questions to specific details to assist the student with the sequencing task.
- Student describes and places Picture Sequence Cards in an order, from first to last.
- Student touches each sequence card to verbalize the story.
- Begin with two Picture Sequence Cards and extend up to five cards.

Visualizing and Verbalizing Picture Stories

With the student able to verbally describe each picture card, sequence the cards, and then tell a story, the instruction adds direct stimulation of imagery. After touching each picture and verbalizing the story sequence, the student turns over the cards and reverbalizes from his imagery-recall.

Here is Miss Billie with Chip after he has sequenced and verbalized a picture story from three picture cards.

S A M P L E L E S S O N

Visualizing and Verbalizing Picture Stories

Billie: "Now touch each picture and tell me the story they make. Start here with the first picture."

Chip: "The big brown and white dog is dirty. Mud puddle. Girl give dog a bath. Dog is clean."

Billie: "Great. That is a good story to picture. Now look at each picture carefully. Then put the cards to sleep."

Chip: He turns over each card.

Billie: "Touch the first card and tell me the story again. Use the pictures in your head. When you're all done, you can wake the cards up and see how you did."

Chip: "Brown and white dog in mud puddle. He dirty. He is dirty. Little girl got water on him. Bath. The dog is clean." He touches each picture as he tells about it.

Billie: "You are great, Chip. You are great! Wake them up and see how you did!"

Lesson Summary:
Visualizing and Verbalizing Picture Stories

- Teacher places Picture Sequence Cards in random order for the student to describe.
- Teacher questions to specific details to assist the student with the sequencing task.
- Student describes and places sequence cards in order from first to last.
- Student touches each sequence card to verbalize the story.
- Student puts the sequence cards to "sleep" by turning the cards over.
- Student touches each sequence card and reverbalizes the story sequence from his own imagery-recall.
- If needed, let the student peek at a card to trigger imagery and recall.
- Extend the Talking Picture Stories lessons to four and five cards.

You may need to let the student peek at a card to refresh his imagery-recall. Also, you may decide to start the imagery with only two cards. Remember, you are the diagnostician. All these lessons with Miss Billie were included to help you experience not only the lesson interaction but also the parts-to-whole nature of *Talkies*.

Error Handling

Talkies students often have difficulty with the concept sequence, whether putting the pictures in order or verbalizing the story back in a sequential order. Here Chip verbally summarizes his imagery for the pictures, but when he can't recall the last picture, he says nothing.

SAMPLE LESSON

Visualizing and Verbalizing Picture Stories

ERROR: When summarizing his story, Chip forgets the last picture.

Billie: "Now touch each picture and tell me the story of them. Start here with the first picture."

Chip: "The big brown and white dog is dirty. Girl give dog a bath...." Chip stops with his hand on the third picture, but doesn't say anything.

Billie: "You are right. First we saw the big brown and white dog dirty in the mud puddle and next we saw the girl give the dog a bath. What did you picture for the very last thing we saw?" Miss Billie notices he is looking up with his eyes, imaging, and she gives him time to bring back the image before she asks any more questions. "This is the one we saw the dog with no dirt, he was...."

Chip: "The dog is clean!"

Billie: "Great job, you got it! Now the dog is clean after his bath."

Practice and Pacing

Talking Picture Stories is about developing visualizing and verbalizing, not just verbalizing, which is often the primary focus in the use of sequence cards. This step requires consistent reinforcement, and is to be included in your overlapping plan. Practice and drive the sensory bus with your questions. Make his sensory system create images.

When this level becomes more automatic and the student is consistently able to visualize and verbalize a three-card story, he is prepared for the next step of Simple Sentence by Sentence. In Sentence by Sentence instruction, the student creates gestalt imagery from language, not given pictures, and summarizes his imagery in a word summary. He is nearing the end of *Talkies*, the *V/V* primer, and getting ready to enter *V/V* at the Sentence by Sentence level.

Summary: Step 8

Talking Picture Stories

Goal: The goal is to develop gestalt imagery from given pictures and extend expressive language into a story summary.

1. Sequencing Picture Stories

- Teacher checks to be sure the student has mastery of the concepts *first* and *last*.
- Teacher places Picture Sequence Cards in random order for the student to describe.
- Teacher questions to specific details to assist the student with the sequencing task.
- Student describes and places sequence cards in order, from first to last.
- Student touches each sequence card to verbalize the story.
- Begin with two Picture Sequence Cards and extend up to five cards.

2. Visualizing and Verbalizing Picture Stories

- Teacher places Picture Sequence Cards in random order for the student to describe.
- Teacher questions to specific details to assist the student with the sequencing task.
- Student describes and places sequence cards in order from first to last.
- Student touches each sequence card to verbalize the story.
- Student puts the sequence cards to "sleep" by turning the cards over.
- Student touches each sequence card and reverbalizes the story sequence from his own imagery-recall.
- If needed, let the student peek at a card to trigger imagery and recall.
- Extend the Talking Picture Stories lessons to four and five cards.

Group Instruction

As in previous steps, adapt Talking Picture Stories to a group by having the students work on the lesson together. Encourage the group to respond nonverbally to student responses, and question students randomly, to make sure all stay attentive and involved. When summarizing the picture story, have different students come forward to touch the cards and tell what happened next.

13 Simple Sentence by Sentence

The goal of Simple Sentence by Sentence is to develop the student's ability to create an imaged gestalt from language in order to provide sensory information for a detailed, sequential verbal summary of the expressed concepts. All previous steps have been preparation for this step, the last sensory domino in our *V/V* primer.

In Simple Sentence by Sentence instruction, the student creates gestalt imagery from language and summarizes his imagery in a word summary. He is nearing the end of *Talkies* and getting ready to enter *V/V* at the Sentence by Sentence level. This will extend his critical thinking skills and prepare him for multiple sentence imagery, whole paragraph imagery, and so on, until he is able to dual code and think critically from extended amounts of oral and written language.

Successful at Talking Picture Stories, your student now creates his own imaged sequential pictures from language, one sentence at a time. Each sentence becomes a picture card created by his own mental imagery of the language. Simple connected sentences are imaged, sequenced, and dual coded with verbal descriptions of each sentence.

At the single sentence level, the student imaged the parts—the words—and created the whole of a sentence. At the Simple Sentence by Sentence level, the student images new parts—the sentences—and creates the whole of a paragraph. The sentences are high in imagery, using concepts your student is familiar with rather than trying to teach new vocabulary or new basic concepts. The goal is to have the student visualize and verbalize a gestalt, the most important achievement in *Talkies*.

A Look at Chip Now

Chip has continued to blossom. Day after day, he does just a little bit better with expressive language. He has taken some big steps and also some little steps. He often speaks in complete, fluent sentences, and he rarely reverts back to being the hidden child, alone in a crowd. He usually participates because he usually expresses himself well enough to be understood. He follows simple directions, especially when encouraged to picture what is being said before doing it. He plays with other children, not just alone. He seems happy and less frustrated. He exhibits reciprocity and emotional responsiveness to peers and adults.

Chip is now beginning the last step of *Talkies* and Miss Billie is watching him closely for faster mental imaging and lengthier verbal expressions where he connects more and more thoughts together. She is aware that the Simple Sentence by Sentence step will assist him with the latter, and she is consciously watching for it. Her sessions with Chip have become a high point in her day. She loves to see his little head come in the door. She loves to see him smile when he is successful. She loves to see him trying to share with her something that happened to him. Now, about to start the last step of *Talkies*, she is already starting to worry that his parents will stop bringing him before they can do *V/V* together.

Simple Sentence by Sentence Imaging

In this step, the student creates an imaged gestalt from simple sentences. The high-imagery sentences are connected one to the other, resulting in a high-imagery paragraph. Paragraph samples are included in the *Talkies* Word and Sentence Reference. The student visualizes and verbalizes each sentence in the paragraph and then places a colored square on the table to represent his imagery. The Picture Structure Words may be used for each sentence, helping to build detailed imagery and verbalization.

The teacher touches each colored square and gives a picture summary by verbally describing the sentence-imagery. The student judges right or wrong. Sometimes the teacher prompts the student to contribute to the picture summary by giving him imagery clues and pausing to help him recall and verbalize his imagery.

With the picture summary complete, the teacher collects the colored squares and gives a word summary by verbally summarizing the whole story described by the sentences. Again, the student judges right or wrong. As before, the teacher sometimes prompts the student to contribute with imagery clues, giving him time to recall his imagery and verbalize it.

As the student begins to visualize and verbalize with fewer prompts from the teacher, the lessons will grow shorter. At that time, the student may check through the structure words to reverbalize his imagery. It is important to note that the act of checking through the structure words develops expressive language because the student has to *reverbalize* his imagery. Not only does reverbalizing through the structure words give him additional practice in expressive language, it also assists him in establishing more *fluent* verbalization, since he is reverbalizing something he has previously imaged and described.

Here are the Simple Sentence by Sentence steps:

1. The teacher says a simple, high-imagery sentence to the student.
2. The student places a colored square on the table as an anchor for his sentence-imagery, and then visualizes and verbalizes the sentence.
3. The sentence has words the student is familiar with, which may elicit sound effects to enhance imagery.
4. The teacher questions his imagery with choice and contrast, keeping in mind the importance of questioning to the gestalt.
5. The teacher questions to the main character or concept first, and then to the familiar structure words.
6. The student may check through some of the Picture Structure Words to develop detailed imagery for each sentence.
7. The teacher says the next sentences and directs the student to form a gestalt with his imagery, not just separate, unrelated parts.
8. The student places colored squares for each sentence and then visualizes and verbalizes the sentence.
9. The student goes through the two- to three-sentence paragraph sentence by sentence.

10. The teacher touches each square and gives a picture summary by verbally describing the images the student created for each sentence. The student judges right or wrong.

11. The teacher prompts the student to contribute to the picture summary by giving him imagery clues and pausing to help him recall and verbalize his imagery.

12. The teacher collects the colored squares and together she and the student give a word summary by verbally summarizing the whole paragraph.

In the lesson below, Miss Billie overlaps Chip from Talking Picture Stories where the pictures were given to him, to a step where she has him create his own mental pictures to sequence and verbalize. She rewards him as usual, but in the interest of brevity, as in some prior lessons, that interaction is not included below. Let's listen in and watch her develop his imagery with her questions.

Simple Sentence by Sentence

Billie: "You can tell me a story when we use pictures. This time you're going to make your own pictures—in your mind! You can do a whole movie up there! Grab two squares for us!"

Chip: He gets a red square and a yellow square, ready to go, his big eyes looking at Miss Billie, a smile on his face. "Okay. I'm ready!"

Billie: "Great. Picture this: *The cat jumped out of the big tree.* What did those words make you picture? Tell me everything you can."

Chip: "The cat. Cat jumped."

Billie: "Right! Get a colored square for your picture." She helps him place the colored square in front of him. "The words make us picture a cat, and the cat jumped. Let's

picture the cat better. What color is your cat? White? Orange? Black? Go through your structure words." She puts the Picture Structure Words out in front of him to help him get the details.

Chip: "The cat is orange. He is big." He touches the *color* and *size* structure words.

Billie: "What do you picture for the cat's head? Does he have eyes and ears?"

Chip: "Yes. He has ears."

Billie: Knowing not to assume imagery, she questions Chip's response to be sure he is visualizing and not just saying the words back. "What size do you picture his ears? Are they little like this or big like this?"

Chip: "Little ears." He smiles.

Billie: "Show me with your hands how little his ears are. Are they like this or like this?"

Chip: "This." He shows little ears.

Billie: "Great! Good picturing. What do you picture for his eyes? Big eyes or—?"

Chip: "Little eyes. He has little eyes. His eyes are blue."

Billie: "Wow! Great picturing. Let's picture more of the cat. What about his fur and his tail?"

Miss Billie continues to question Chip to develop his image of the cat. But she knows to move on, so as not to tire Chip; thus, she doesn't get so much detail that she loses the energy of the lesson or his much-needed attention. We'll look in after she has had him picture the cat and the cat jumping.

Billie: "Great job on the cat and the cat jumping. See if there is anything else we need to picture.

The cat jumped out of the big tree. What else do you have to put in your picture?"

Chip: "A tree?"

Billie: "Right, a tree. What size is the tree? A big tree or a little tree?"

Chip: "A big tree."

Billie: "Yes! How big do you picture the tree? Is it as big as this room? Or is it big like that door?" She uses a reference in the room to help him picture.

Chip: "It is big like this room. Big!"

After more interaction Miss Billie believes Chip is picturing the sentence now, not just saying the words back to her. She has him add a sound effect for the cat to enhance his imagery a little bit more.

Billie: "What sound can we picture for the cat?"

Chip: "Meow."

Billie: "Right. Make a big loud meow." She asks him to exaggerate the sound to make his imagery even more vivid.

Chip: "MEOW!"

Billie: "Let's do one more sentence. Picture this: *The cat fell into a swimming pool.* Put this square down. What do those words make you picture? *The cat fell into a swimming pool.*"

Chip: "Cat in the water. He went in water!"

Billie: "Right! Keep your same orange cat from before. What does he look like now?"

Chip: "He is in the water. He is wet."

Billie: "Right! I can picture his fur all wet and stuck to him." She helps him visualize by adding some elements and continues questioning him. "What did you picture for the water? The words said *The cat fell into a swimming pool.* What do you picture for the swimming pool?"

Chip: "Water. I see blue water."

Miss Billie and Chip only work on his imagery a little bit longer. They do not go through all the structure words because it would make the lesson too long. She touches each colored square and gives a picture summary. Sometimes he judges right or wrong (receptive practice) and sometimes she asks him to verbalize (expressive practice) part of the summary as she gives him imagery clues to help him recall his picture.

Billie: "Now I'm going to touch each square and tell you what we pictured. You tell me if I'm right or wrong, thumbs-up or down." She touches the first colored square. "Here we saw...." She verbalizes most of their pictures and then asks Chip for a part.

Billie: "What did we picture for his sound?"

Chip: "MEOW!"

Billie: "Right." She laughs as she touches the second square. "Here we saw...." She again verbalizes most of the imagery, but asks Chip for some parts.

Billie: "What did we picture for the swimming pool?"

Chip: "Water. The water is blue. And the cat in it! He is wet."

Billie: "Right! Here we saw the cat fall in the water in the swimming pool and he was all wet. Pick up all the colored squares and I'll tell you the whole thing we pictured."

Chip: He picks up the squares.

Billie: "You see if I can tell us everything in our picture story. Give me thumbs-up or thumbs-down. Okay?"

Chip: "Okay."

Billie: "This was about how a cat jumped off a…." She pauses to see if he can fill in.

Chip: "A tree. The cat jumped off a tree."

Billie: "Right! And he fell into…." She pauses to see if he can fill it in again.

Chip: "Water. He fell in the swimming pool."

Lesson Summary:
Simple Sentence by Sentence

- Teacher says a simple, high-imagery sentence to the student.
- Student places a colored square on the table as an anchor for his sentence-imagery, and then visualizes and verbalizes the sentence.
- The sentence has words the student is familiar with, which may elicit sound effects to enhance imagery.
- Teacher questions his imagery with choice and contrast, keeping in mind the importance of questioning to the gestalt.
- Teacher questions to the main character or concept first, and then to the familiar structure words.
- Student may check through some of the Picture Structure Words to develop detailed imagery for each sentence.
- Teacher says the next sentences and directs student to form a gestalt with his imagery, not just separate, unrelated parts.
- Student places colored squares for each sentence and then visualizes and verbalizes the sentence.
- Student goes through the two- to three-sentence paragraph sentence by sentence.
- Teacher touches each square and gives a picture summary by verbally describing the images the student created for each sentence. The student judges right or wrong.
- Teacher prompts student to contribute to the picture summary by giving him imagery clues and pausing to help him recall and verbalize his imagery.
- Teacher collects the colored squares and together she and the student give a word summary by verbally summarizing the whole paragraph.

Important Elements of Sentence by Sentence

Since this is the last step of *Talkies* and the second most important part of the entire program, it is important to understand its nuances.

1. Receptive Language Stimulation:

   Simple Sentence by Sentence stimulation is always verbal in *Talkies*, whereas in *V/V* the language may be presented in oral or written form.

2. Begin with Two Sentences and Extend to Four Sentences:

   Simple Sentence by Sentence stimulation begins with words the student knows and can perhaps give a sound effect for, gesture, or act out. The stimulation also begins with just two sentences, moves to three, and concludes with four sentences. Simple sentences and Sentence by Sentence samples are in the *Talkies* Word and Sentence Reference.

3. Drive the Sensory Bus for Imagery:

   Follow each sentence with the question, "What do those words make you picture?" Don't assume imagery. Question to be sure your student is imaging, not just saying words back. For example, if you give two choices and the student chooses one of the choices, question to be sure he is visualizing.

   "What did you picture, a little mouse or a big mouse?"

   "Little."

   "What do you picture for a little mouse. Show me with your hands. Are you picturing the mouse little like this (gesturing) or little like this (gesturing again)?"

4. Question Toward the Gestalt:

   Direct your questions to develop imagery for the main idea of the sentences rather than the separate parts.

5. Connect Images from Sentence to Sentence:

   Help the student picture the same central character or activity so his imagery will be connected from sentence to sentence, creating the necessary gestalt.

6. Use the Picture Structure Words for Each Sentence:

   In *Talkies*, the structure words are limited to *what, color, size, shape, movement, number*, and *where*, and they may be used to create detailed imagery and language for each sentence.

7. Placing the Colored Squares:

   The student places a colored square to anchor his imagery before he starts to verbalize. The squares are placed from top to bottom rather than right to left. This is especially important if the student is still doing the Talking Sentences step, where the colored squares represent words in a sentence and are placed left to right.

8. Check Through the Structure Words at the End of the First Sentence:

   Check through the structure words after the first sentence only when the student has gained some success with Sentence by Sentence processing. If you have the student go through each structure word and tell you what he visualized for each of them, your lesson may be too long. Don't do this until you are sure your student won't tire and lose his energy for the lesson.

9. Picture Summary:

   The summary of the sentences begins with a picture summary. In *Talkies*, unlike *V/V*, the teacher is primarily responsible for the verbal summary of each sentence. She and the student touch each colored square and say, "Here we saw…." The teacher verbalizes the sentence-images, pausing to see if the student can contribute to the verbal description for specific images. She puts a Magic Stone on the square every time the student adds to the verbalization. The eventual goal is to have the student do the picture summary without the teacher's assistance.

10. Word Summary:

    A word summary is a verbal summary of the whole paragraph (the connected sentences). Because a word summary is often more difficult than a picture summary, requiring more verbalization and the ability to synthesize and paraphrase, in *Talkies* the teacher gives the word summary with or without the student's help. In both the picture summary and word summary steps, the interaction can be receptive, where the student judges right or wrong, thumbs-up or down. This keeps the student attending, lets you know that he is processing, and can eventually be changed to expressive practice by encouraging the student to verbalize parts of the paragraph.

A picture summary describes images and a word summary paraphrases the entirety of the sentences. Don't mix up the two.

11. Beware of Taking too Long:

    While it is important to develop imagery for each sentence, you must not ask for so much imagery that the student is drained of energy and attention. There is a fine line between asking too few questions and too many questions. The difference lies in your ability to monitor your student's dual coding ability and his energy level. Along with monitoring the lesson energy, remember also to change the learning environment, especially for Sentence by Sentence, to help sustain the student's attention. For example, have the student stand up when he has verbalized an image and then sit down when you indicate thumbs-up. Have him give you one Magic Stone when you verbalize and give himself two Magic Stones when he verbalizes. See how big the pile of stones can grow. Be creative without interrupting the goal of the lesson.

12. Continue to Use Immediate Rewards:

    While not shown in the lessons with Chip, Miss Billie continues to give Chip rewards of Magic Stones, raisins, or bits of popcorn throughout most of their lessons, and he collects prizes on a regular basis.

13. Watch for Signs of Imagery:

    Remember, you are the diagnostician and you are always looking for signs of imagery, and also the vividness and speed of that imagery. Notice whether your student moves his eyes up or defocuses to access his imagery. Notice the speed in which he responds to your questions about imagery. Notice the richness of his imagery; is he adding color and movement? Remember, there are college-age students who have initially described their imagery as dark and colorless, without movement. If that can be the case for those individuals, imagine what might be happening or not happening for a *Talkies* student.

14. How to Correct an Erroneous Image:

    If your student gives you an erroneous image or leaves something out, repeat the stimulus to him. "Let's listen to the words again and see if we want to add or change anything." You may need to call attention to the specific image to be visualized. For example, if the student visualized the cat in a little tree but the language said the cat was in a big tree, you first give positive feedback—that it is good that he visualized a tree. Then call attention to the discrepancy. "Let's check what size tree we should picture. It said the cat was in a big tree. Should we picture a little tree or a big tree?" If the student then chooses "big," you will not assume he imaged "big." Instead, develop his imagery by giving him a reference in the room. "Is it big like this, or like this...?"

Oral Vocabulary Is Necessary for Sentence by Sentence Processing

The importance of oral vocabulary to receptive and expressive language processing becomes especially critical when you reach the Simple Sentence by Sentence step in *Talkies*. Without quick, well-established imagery for the words within the sentence—the parts—the student cannot create more comprehensive mental imagery for the whole. As noted in the chapter "Chip and a Guide," the direct stimulation of oral vocabulary is continued throughout *Talkies*, developing the ability to image the meaning of a word, to store that imaged meaning, and to access and retrieve the meaning more rapidly. While each step of *Talkies* stimulates the student's ability to quickly create mental representations for words, you must still make additional effort to track and extend his individual oral vocabulary in each lesson. You will very likely still be working on oral vocabulary even as you reach this last step of *Talkies*.

Error Handling

Sometimes the speed in which words come at our sensory system may cause a student to miss a part that has to be imaged. Chip is learning to visualize language, but the speed in which he converts language to imagery is still slow. Say sentences at a relatively normal speed, not too slow or too fast. If you say the sentence too slowly, then you are stimulating word imagery but not sentence imagery. Listen as Miss Billie quickly helps him compare his response to the stimulus.

SAMPLE LESSON

Simple Sentence by Sentence

ERROR: Chip didn't visualize the action correctly in the sentence.

Billie: "Great. Picture this: *The cat jumped out of the big tree.* What did those words make you picture? Tell me everything you can."

Chip: "Cat runs."

Billie: "Good. We have to picture a cat. You are picturing the cat run. Show me what *run* would look like. Let's see if that is what the words tell us to picture." She rereads the sentence to him. "*The cat jumped out of the big tree.* Do the words tell us to picture the cat running or—?"

Chip: "Jump. The cat jumped."

Miss Billie can have Chip show her *jump* and then show her *run* to contrast the two movements. Then she can read the sentence again to make sure he hears all the words for this image.

Summary

As you and your student progress through *Talkies*, you can begin to talk to him in longer sentences. You may begin to assume some imagery so your lessons may not be as long and your questioning may not have to be so detailed. Your student will likely be able to express himself better than in the early steps of *Talkies*. Most importantly, you know what you are doing and why you are doing it. Therefore, your questions are more focused, you respond to the response, and your lessons are faster and less cumbersome.

You know about dual coding, the important sensory connection between imagery and language processing. You made it. You have completed the steps of valuable instruction for your student or students.

Summary: Step 9

Simple Sentence by Sentence

Goal: The goal is to begin to develop and verbally describe an imaged gestalt from simple, connected sentences.

1. **Simple Sentence by Sentence**
    - Teacher says a simple, high-imagery sentence to the student.
    - Student places a colored square on the table as an anchor for his sentence-imagery, and then visualizes and verbalizes the sentence.
    - The sentence has words student is familiar with, which may elicit sound effects to enhance imagery.
    - Teacher questions student's imagery with choice and contrast, keeping in mind the importance of questioning to the gestalt.
    - Teacher questions to the main character or concept first, and then to the familiar structure words.
    - Student may check through some of the Picture Structure Words to develop detailed imagery for each sentence.
    - Teacher says the next sentences and directs the student to form a gestalt with his imagery, not just separate, unrelated parts.
    - Student places colored squares for each sentence and then visualizes and verbalizes the sentence.

- Student goes through the two- to three-sentence paragraph sentence by sentence.
- Teacher touches each square and gives a picture summary by verbally describing the images the student created for each sentence. The student judges right or wrong.
- Teacher prompts the student to contribute to the picture summary by giving him imagery clues and pausing to help him recall and verbalize his imagery.
- Teacher collects the colored squares and together she and the student give a word summary by verbally summarizing the whole paragraph.

Group Instruction

Continue to engage the entire group as you visualize and verbalize each sentence by calling randomly on students to describe what they had imaged for each sentence, adding richness to the imagery. Continue to develop imagery through your questioning, and rephrase the student descriptions by saying, "Your words are making us picture...." Once each sentence is complete, you can have the group judge right or wrong with verbal or nonverbal responses. This practice helps close the circle for the students, and helps them apprehend the gestalt of the sentence.

The Summary

14 Autism and Dual Coding

Autism is a complex neurobiological developmental disorder characterized by impaired social interaction, problems with verbal and nonverbal communication, and unusual, repetitive, or severely limited activities and interests.

Over the last few years the number of children diagnosed with an Autism Spectrum Disorder (ASD) has increased at an alarming rate. There has been nearly a 200 percent increase in the reported cases of autism in the last decade, and estimates for the current incidence nationwide vary from 1 in 500 to 1 in 150. An increased awareness of the symptoms of children with disorders in relating and communicating, including ASD, cannot account for such a significant increase in diagnosis. Unfortunately, we lack a clear understanding of the causes and biological pathways involved for children with ASD. It is largely believed that there are numerous causes of these disorders, including genetic and autoimmune factors and environmental toxins. There are also numerous subtypes of the disorders, including many subtypes of ASD perhaps yet to be clearly described.

The complexity of autism cannot be summarized in a chapter in this manual, and that is not our intent. Sitting with Stanley Greenspan's books piled around us, articles from other professionals strewn everywhere we look, along with printouts from the numerous websites that provide information on autism, we believe that any attempt at summary would be misleading, and a disservice. Instead, we will connect dual coding to autism for you.

As was discussed earlier in this manual, the more severe the student's weakness in concept imagery, the more severe the symptoms of difficulty in relating and communicating. These symptoms may even be so severe as to place the student on the autism spectrum. While there are many causes contributing to a diagnosis of ASD, weakness in dual coding—poor integration of imagery and language and the processing of parts-to-whole relationships—is a contributing factor.

The integration of imagery and verbal processing is critical to cognitive processing, something we hope we've expressed throughout this manual. The nonverbal system of imagery provides sensory support for the verbal system with the goal of bringing parts to a whole. Many children on the autistic spectrum have a propensity to process parts. The following are well-documented symptoms of autism, separated into categories that show how they relate to parts-whole processing strengths and weaknesses.

Ability to process parts contributes to strength in:

- Rote memory
- Mechanical tasks
- Acquisition of simple information
- Simple procedural tasks
- Simple associations
- Word recognition skills
- Spelling
- Rote computational tasks
- Short-term, immediate repetition of oral material

Inability to process wholes contributes to weakness in:

- Complex information processing
- Concept formation
- Abstract and critical thinking
- Interpretive oral language comprehension
- Interpretive reading comprehension
- Complex memory for oral and written material
- Following complex oral/written directions
- Problem solving
- Analysis and synthesis of information
- Organizational strategies

It may be thought that autistic children have strength in visual-spatial processing because they can remember a place in a room where a toy has been hidden or because they seem to have a good visual mapping system that helps them remember places. Some have confused that type of visual-spatial processing as an indication that the child has strength in visual imagery as described in *V/V* and *Talkies*. But the visual imagery ability we are discussing is the *dual coding of imagery and language.*

Imagery and Visually Based Material

It has often been noted that children on the autistic spectrum respond well to visually based material in instructional settings because the visual representation makes language and the physical environment more concrete for them. This is a highly effective mode of instruction, in which auditory input is supplemented with visual "backup."

The following list illustrates the benefits of using visually based material to supplement auditory information (Twachtman-Cullen, 1998). However, note that in each case visual imagery can be substituted for visually based material and offer children an *internal* visual backup system.

- Visually based material is stable over time. *Visual imagery is stable over time and internal for children, enabling them to have access to their own internal visual backup at a conscious level anywhere, at anytime.*
- By supplementing the auditory channel with visual back up, the individual has the benefit of two input channels. *By supplementing the auditory channel with visual imagery, the individual can integrate verbal and nonverbal sensory information, anywhere, at anytime.*
- Visual information is an "eye catcher" for capturing and maintaining attention. *Visual imagery is also an eye-catcher, only it is internal, enabling the individual to attend and focus even when eye-catching external material is absent.*
- Visual supplementation aids processing ability. *Given that visual imagery is the nonverbal code for dual coding, visual imagery aids processing ability and is available at a conscious and unconscious level to the individual anywhere, at anytime.*
- Visual information helps make concepts more understandable by making

them concrete. *Visual imagery concretizes language with sensory information that can be internally manipulated, related, stored, and retrieved.*

- Visual information can increase understanding in general. *Visual imagery for the gestalt enables individuals to process concepts anywhere, at anytime.*
- Visual supports can be used to prompt individuals. *Visual imagery can be used to prompt individuals through conscious questioning of imagery relevant to the event or concept, or through individuals' own internal "prompt," which allows them to contrast and compare with imagery.*
- Visual supports can help minimize anxiety. *Visual imagery for concepts helps minimize anxiety by making the communicating world seem less like a jumble of random parts. With an imaged gestalt, meaning can be derived from both oral and written language.*
- Visual supports can render information more memorable. *As research shows, imagery is related to memory and recall; hence, visual imagery renders information more memorable.*

Visual backup is helpful and effective but it is not with your student all the time. Visual imagery is an internal sensory reality that can be developed and eventually substituted for visual aids in the classroom or at home. As imagery resides within the child, independence is developed for crossover to many social situations.

Dual Coding for Floortime, Play, and Pragmatics

During Floortime activities and play, imagery can be specifically stimulated with questions that draw attention to mental representations for actions or events. It is important for you to become part of the child's team of professionals so you can directly help him integrate the many techniques that are being used with him. For example, in Floortime, a reference to imagery can become part of the language between the therapist and the child. Following the child's lead, say, "I'm picturing that the horse is going to fall off the wall. What are you picturing? Let's picture it and do it." Even if imagery cannot be brought to a conscious level for the child, the reference to it as a cognitive tool is better than saying, "I'm thinking that the horse is going to fall off the wall. What are you thinking?" The word *thinking* doesn't have a sensory connection for the child, whereas the word *picturing* does. Even if the child is responding minimally to language, it is important to connect the concrete activity of play to the concreteness of imagery, helping move the child to symbolic play based on mental-representation ability. The more absurd the play and imagery, the more contrast there is, and the more likely the child will begin to engage and begin to make the play-imagery-language connection.

As the play interaction progresses, extend the play-imagery-language stimulation to making predictions and thinking abstractly, as in, "If our big tractor runs into this little fence, what do you picture will happen to the fence? Let's see if what you pictured really happens." Verify the imagery with action and use language to describe both. Again, language such as, "What do you think will happen..." or "What do you remember..." doesn't call attention to sensory information because *think* and *remember* are abstract.

For pragmatics, the play-imagery-language interaction can be used in connection with both *Talkies* and *V/V*. Using imagery for pragmatics requires the child to be able to image the gestalt as a means of vicariously experiencing social situations and determining appropriate reactions. The child can visualize the setting and the characters of a given situation and then visualize different actions and reactions. Imagery is used to interpret the situation, the cause of the event, and the appropriate and/or inappropriate reactions or responses. From the imagery, inferences, conclusions, and predictions can be made, allowing the child to practice without being in a social situation that may become a negative experience.

Summary

While important knowledge has been gained about the imagery-language connection to parts-whole processing and children on the autistic spectrum, there are many challenges yet to be met. For example, tests for imagery need to be developed and fMRI studies need to be conducted to measure the brain's processing ability before and after an intervention to specifically stimulate dual coding.

If the greatest thinkers of our time attribute their strength in cognitive ability to imagery, it is reasonable conversely to think that weakness in cognitive ability is related to weakness in imagery. Developing the imagery-language connection for children may contribute to our continuing effort to bring children from the darkness into the light.

15 Who Is a *Talkies* Student?

Talkies is a program for both remedial and developmental instruction. Remedially, *Talkies* is appropriate for a student of any age with two specific areas of weakness: poor oral vocabulary and delayed receptive/expressive language. Developmentally, *Talkies* is beneficial for all young children between the ages of two and five, preschool through kindergarten, and perhaps into first grade. All young children are *Talkies* students because it is important to develop dual coding at a conscious level at the earliest ages possible to prevent language processing delays at a later age.

Students must be carefully diagnosed before being placed in remedial instruction in *Talkies*. Some students need basic *V/V*, not *Talkies*, and placing them in *Talkies* when they only need *V/V* wastes precious instruction time. So who are *Talkies* students and what are the challenges they face?

Students of any age may benefit from *Talkies* if they have severe weakness in receptive and expressive oral vocabulary (below the 25th percentile) and demonstrate substantial weakness in receptive/expressive oral language. Before Chip, there were other girls and boys, young and old, who came to us for help. Many were referrals from professionals across the United States who work with children on the autistic spectrum. Some children were very young, some were on the autistic spectrum, and some had not yet been diagnosed.

There were little girls like eight-year-old Shannon, who was described as shy and possibly on the autistic spectrum. Shannon only spoke to her parents, always with her head down and very little eye contact, and with only one or two words in each sentence. Her receptive and expressive oral vocabulary tested below the 1st percentile.

There was Trevor, an eight-year-old boy, hyperlexic and diagnosed autistic, who only spoke in two- to four-word sentences even after years of traditional speech therapy. His receptive and expressive oral vocabulary tested below the 25th percentile.

There was Jordan, the severely autistic fourteen-year-old girl, who had experienced numerous types of speech, behavioral, and medical interventions since she was a young child. Many professionals across the country were following her progress and interacting with her parents. She didn't talk or understand language when we met her as a teenager, saying only a few irrelevant words and striking out with poor behavior. Her oral vocabulary tested below the 1st percentile.

There was Maggie, a five year old, who responded with the appropriate tones and rhythms of language, but in reality her language was more like a stream of consciousness, unrelated and irrelevant, much like the babbling of a one year old. Her oral vocabulary and basic concepts were severely impaired.

There were more. They kept coming to our clinics because *V/V* had helped many children who had trouble with oral and written language comprehension and expression. We began to chip away at the marble, putting steps in a sequence, taking *V/V* back to the most basic levels to consciously develop imagery as a sensory tool for language acquisition and expression.

Developing imagery was not going to be an easy task since it was evident that imagery was not at a conscious level for these children, not vivid, not quickly created or accessed, and not integrating with language. Imagery wouldn't easily be stimulated or integrated. Even after years of speech therapy, the weakness in oral vocabulary for such basic language concepts as *up* and *down*, *in* and *out*, was often significant for these children. Telling a child to "picture in his mind" was not going to be effective. Along with language weakness, eye contact was often minimal; if there was eye contact it appeared distant, representing a social reflex rather than a cognitive response. The children seemed interiorized.

Other abilities, such as small and large motor planning, had often developed for these children, but imagery—half of the dual code—had not. One could speculate that as words were being heard in the early years of language development, they did not connect to anything concrete because of a weakness in imagery ability. The words were not being concretized by imagery. And the snowball effect ensued. If the connections of words/language to imagery were not made at an early age, then language could not easily be attached, organized, categorized, or generated from and to other areas. Vocabulary was weakened because images had not connected to the developing language. Since single-word vocabulary was deficient, organized and connected thought was severely impacted. Processing was slow and a moment of connection with oral language, such as in conversation, often came and went. With the connection gone, even more language poured in, unable to be processed. Sometimes the frustration and pain resulted in interiorized behavior that replaced understanding and connections to family and peers—and the rest of the communicating world. Sometimes the frustration resulted in externalized, aggressive behavior with little understanding of cause and effect and little processing of language that might help change the behavior. Tantrums and tears led to a potentially damaged self-image and emotional issues in the affective domain. One half of a code, a weakened sensory input, caused significant problems. This imagery would need to be *stimulated* rather than compensated for, as too often happens when the educational profession doesn't know how to correct a specific weakness.

Imagery had to be developed and these students became *Talkies* students—students you now know how to help.

How do you know the difference between a Talkies student and a V/V Student?

Even a label such as autism may not automatically place a student in *Talkies* instead of *V/V*. Rather than prescribe instructional placement based on a label, monitor the student's learning profile for severe weaknesses in oral vocabulary and receptive/expressive language—and his response to instruction.

Here is a young boy who wasn't a *Talkies* student, though he had been labeled autistic, had undergone years of speech therapy, and was now in a special day class. Marcus was a ten-year-old hyperlexic, reading at an extraordinarily high level before he was five years old. However, his parents reported that he could only read the words; he had no comprehension of what he decoded. They had an enormous file documenting years of professional diagnoses and consultations, including the speech therapy that began when he was three years old. Now at age ten, he could talk but it was limited, and while he made eye contact and engaged, he still appeared withdrawn. Our diagnostic evaluation noted that Marcus's paragraph reading accuracy and fluency were above the 99th percentile but his reading comprehension was below the 1st percentile. Given just that amount of diagnostic information, one might have thought he was a *Talkies* student. However, our diagnostic testing also noted that Marcus had receptive oral vocabulary at the 75th percentile and his expressive oral vocabulary was at the 37th percentile (word opposites). He was verbal, but not talkative.

We did *V/V* intensively with Marcus, four hours a day, for approximately eight weeks (160 hours). He became more "talkative" and his reading comprehension improved from below the 1st percentile to the 50th percentile. At the completion of the *V/V* intervention, Marcus was able to create mental representations for language and use that imagery to assist him with verbalization. However, his imagery was still not fast enough. He needed more *V/V* in order to reach that threshold level of automaticity in dual coding, and doing the early steps of *Talkies* would have used up precious instruction time with little benefit.

There are many students like Marcus that could benefit from just *V/V* or perhaps even from some of the most crucial steps in *Talkies*, such as Talking Sentences. You have numerous options, but they all begin with diagnostic information, whether that information comes from standardized tests and screenings, or from your own keen observation. For example, rather than placing all severe students in *Talkies*, you can begin with *V/V*, and if your student isn't responding, back up and begin *Talkies*, moving quickly through the early steps. In any case, remember: you are the diagnostician. You know what you are doing and why.

Summary

Imagery is a physical sensory reality for language comprehension and language expressions. As the sensory information of imagery is brought to consciousness, students can access it as a sensory tool, a tool in their cognitive tool box. You now know what to do to develop the imagery-language connection. You know why you are doing it, and you know how to pace your student. You have the knowledge to bring children into the light of communication.

You can do this. You can do anything.

16 What Happened to Chip?

Many weeks have gone by. Chip and Miss Billie work everyday, continuing to image and track vocabulary words, and to visualize and verbalize language. After successfully extending to three and four sentences in the Simple Sentence by Sentence step, Miss Billie transitioned Chip to *V/V* a few weeks ago when she noted that he was able to verbalize a picture summary without prompting from her.

The first thing Miss Billie did with Chip in *V/V* was teach him the remaining *V/V* structure words, providing him with more details for his imagery and verbal descriptions. Since *Talkies* uses only seven of the twelve *V/V* Structure Words, she introduced the remaining structure words to him—*background, when, mood, perspective,* and *sound*—to use in the Picture to Picture, Word Imaging, and Sentence by Sentence steps of *V/V*. Within a week, she noticed that his imagery and verbalization were richer with his conscious attention to the additional descriptors of the added structure words. He began to add mood and background to his imagery and verbal descriptions, and soon added some sound to the what he pictured and described. He was flying.

Life has changed for Chip since that first step with Miss Billie five months ago. He consistently uses appropriate articles, pronouns, prepositions, and verb tenses in his oral language expression, which is consistently sequential and often quite lengthy.

Chip sometimes seems shy, but he understands and expresses language and he participates in conversation at home and at school. He is a little person with a little personality that seems to grow brighter every day. He has funny little things he does, such as smiling with his head down when something amuses him or looking at you with exaggeratedly big eyes when something surprises him.

Miss Billie believes that Chip's dual coding has reached a level of automaticity and therefore it will likely continue to develop without direct stimulation. She sees that Chip processes language not only when being talked to directly, but also when he overhears conversation. A few days ago, she observed him playing with some children and he commented on something they were discussing even though they weren't directly talking to him. He seemed unable to turn his language processing off, whereas a few months ago he seemed unable to turn it on. "Imagery, oh that imagery," she thought.

Last week, Chip's mother came in to talk with Miss Billie. She told Miss Billie that Chip is a chatterbox at home and they are thrilled. She was emotional. "He talks all the time, about everything, what he did at school, who said what...we can't believe it. It is like a miracle. We feel like we are just getting to know this little boy." Then she told Miss Billie that Chip's last day would be next week.

That day has arrived. Chip's last day. Miss Billie is both sad and happy. She won't see him run into the room any more, smiling and reaching out to hold her hand. She won't see him look at her in the way that only an innocent child can look at someone. She won't hear his laugh or see his smile any more. Then, as she is getting some of their books from the shelf, she hears the door open. There he is, and he has flowers in his hand.

"Come on. Let's go read. Oh, these are for you. I'm going on a trip today. We're going to visit my Grandma. She is really old...her hair is gray...and she wears little glasses, like this...she laughs really loud, like this...she lives in a big house...and she has a big cat...and...."

Holding his little hand really tight, Miss Billie whispers, "Thank you, Chip. I'm listening. I'm listening to every word."

The Appendix

Summary: Step 1

Climate

Goal: To briefly explain to the student *what* and *why*.

1. Set the Climate

- Make a head with a thought bubble, then draw the tree as you explain:
- "We will picture words in your mind."
- "We can say *tree*."
- "We can picture a tree."

Summary: Step 2

Sensory-Language Play

Goal: Engage the student, establish reciprocity, and begin an awareness of the imagery-language connection. Following the student's lead, imagery and language are introduced and extended into receptive and expressive play with nonverbal and verbal responses.

1. Play to Establish Rapport

- Student is encouraged to "play" with toys.
- Student begins to be comfortable with the environment.
- Student begins to be comfortable with teacher.
- Teacher notes reciprocity and affective processing.

2. Object Imagery: Touching and Gesturing

- Student is given a simple, known object.
- Student feels the object with his eyes open and then closed.
- With the object taken away, the student gestures the object's size and shape.
- Teacher may help the student gesture.

3. Receptive Play with Thumbs-Up or Thumbs-Down Nonverbal Response

- Student learns nonverbal thumbs-up or thumbs-down gesture, or uses thumbs-up or thumbs-down cards.
- Using a toy, the teacher visualizes, verbalizes, and does an action.
- Student judges right or wrong with thumbs-up or thumbs-down gesture, or card.

4. Receptive Play with Verbal Response

- Using a toy, teacher visualizes, verbalizes, and does an action.
- Student can verbalize *right, wrong, up, down, yes, or no.*
- Student may also use nonverbal thumbs up or thumbs-down gesture.

5. Expressive Play with Action, Nonverbal, and Verbal Responses

a. Expressive Play #1: Teacher Talks and Student Does

- Using a toy, the teacher visualizes, verbalizes, and does.
- Student judges right or wrong, verbally and nonverbally.
- Student pictures the action and does it too.

b. Expressive Play #2: Teacher Does and Student Talks

- Using a toy, the teacher visualizes, verbalizes, and does an action.
- Student verbalizes the action.
- Student does the action.

c. Expressive Play #3: Student Talks and Does

- Student pictures, talks, and does.
- Student takes a toy and says what action he will make the toy do.
- Student does the action with the toy.

Group Instruction

The process of the Sensory-Language Play step requires no modification for small group or classroom instruction, but as in all group instruction, group management techniques need to be employed.

- When first playing to build rapport, encourage all the students to play with the toys and then engage with each individual in turn.
- In Object Imagery, have the students take turns with the object, feeling it, imaging it, and gesturing to their image.
- In Receptive Play with Nonverbal Response, have all the students respond with a thumbs-up or thumbs-down gesture, and then question various students to ensure his or her responses are appropriate.
- In the Receptive and Expressive Play with Verbal Response, all students can respond nonverbally with a thumbs-up or thumbs-down while they take turns giving verbal responses.

Suggested Books and Products

The following books and products are suggested for vocabulary and concept development:

First Concepts Numbers by Robert Tarnish

First Concepts Opposites by Melanie Whittington

Language Builder Picture Cards by Stages® Learning Materials

Learning Block Books, 26 Board Books in a Box! illustrated by Susan Estelle Kwas and designed by Paul Kepple

My Big Animal Book by Roger Priddy

My Little Word Book by Roger Priddy

Scholastic First Picture Dictionary by Geneviève de la Bretesche and illustrated by Charlotte Voake

Slide 'N' Seek Opposites by Chuck Murphy

Summary: Step 3
Talking Words

Goal: Develop imagery for oral vocabulary and basic concepts, and increase word retrieval for expressive language.

1. **Introduce Picture Structure Words**
   - Teacher names a structure word.
   - Student finds and touches the appropriate card.
   - Teacher concretizes the structure word with toys, movements, and contrast.

2. **Receptive Practice with *Picturing Vocabulary!* Cards**
   - Teacher says the name of one card.
   - Teacher encourages the student to picture the word.
   - Student identifies the word by touching the card.
   - Student puts the card to "sleep."

3. **Expressive Practice with *Picturing Vocabulary!* Cards**
   - Teacher puts out the *Picturing Vocabulary!* Cards.
   - Teacher touches a card.

- Student says the name of the card.
- Teacher encourages the student to picture the word.
- Student puts the card to "sleep" and "wakes" it up by naming it.

4. Picture Imagery Practice

- Teacher shows a *Picturing Vocabulary!* Card to the student for approximately two seconds.
- Teacher takes the card away.
- Student recalls his imagery and names the card.
- Teacher asks for specifics like *color, size,* or *movement.*
- Teacher may show the card again to stimulate imagery-recall for details.

5. Take a Step for Picture Imagery Practice

- Student stands a few feet away from the teacher.
- Teacher shows a *Picturing Vocabulary!* Card to the student for approximately two seconds.
- Teacher takes the card away.
- Student recalls his imagery and names the card.
- If accurate, the student takes a step.
- Teacher asks for specifics like *color, shape,* or *size.*
- Student takes additional steps if he can picture/recall details.
- Teacher may show the card again to stimulate imagery-recall for details.

6. Receptive Practice for Vocabulary within Categories

- Teacher introduces the student to categories of words.
- Teacher names a picture within the category.
- Teacher encourages the student to picture the word.

- Student touches the picture of the word, putting a Magic Stone on it.
- Teacher names the common attributes in the category (such as farm animals have legs, eyes, and ears).
- Student touches or puts a stone on the attribute.

7. Expressive Practice for Vocabulary within Categories

- Teacher touches the picture within the category.
- Student names the picture.
- Student puts a Magic Stone on the picture, if named correctly.
- Teacher names the common attributes of the pictures in the category.
- Teacher touches an attribute and the student names it.
- Teacher refers to imagery.

8. Imagery Practice for Vocabulary within Categories

- Teacher shows a page of pictures to the student for approximately two to four seconds.
- Student recalls his imagery and names as many pictures as he can from the page.
- Teacher looks for signs that the student is imaging language.
- Teacher shows the student the page again.
- Teacher and the student point and name the pictures not imaged and recalled.

9. Receptive Practice with Magic Window and Picture Structure Words

- Teacher introduces the student to Magic Window.
- Teacher moves the Magic Window around on a page.
- Teacher names the picture in the hole of the Magic Window.
- Student gives thumbs-up or thumbs-down gesture.
- Teacher and the student check through the structure words.

- Student puts the structure word cards to "sleep" if teacher names that specific attribute of the picture.
- Teacher may discuss and name the common attributes in the category.

10. Expressive Practice with Magic Window and Picture Structure Words

- Teacher moves the Magic Window around on a page.
- Student names the picture in the hole of the Magic Window.
- Student checks through the structure words.
- Student puts the structure word cards to "sleep" as he verbalizes a specific attribute of the picture.
- Teacher may discuss and name the common attributes in the category.
- Teacher continues to refer to imagery.

11. Receptive Practice with Magic Glass

- Teacher introduces the student to Magic Glass.
- Teacher moves the Magic Glass around on a picture.
- Teacher names the picture in the hole of the Magic Glass.
- Student gives thumbs-up or thumbs-down gesture.
- Teacher and the student may check through the structure words.
- Student puts the structure word cards to "sleep" if the teacher names that specific attribute of the picture.

12. Expressive Practice with Magic Glass

- Student moves the Magic Glass around on a picture.
- Student names the picture in the hole of the Magic Glass.
- Student may check through the structure words.
- Teacher names common attributes in a category.

13. Imagery Practice with Magic Glass

- Teacher puts the Magic Glass on a part of a picture for approximately two seconds.
- Student recalls his imagery and names what he recalls (images).
- Teacher looks for signs that the student is accessing imagery.
- Teacher shows the student the picture and they discuss details of the picture that they may have missed.

14. Imagery Practice with Magic Bag: Student Uses Magic Hands to Feel, Image, and Describe

- Teacher puts two or three toys in the Magic Bag.
- Student feels inside the bag.
- Student feels, images, and names the toy he chooses to describe.
- Teacher looks for signs that the student is accessing imagery.
- Student takes the toy he described out of the bag to see if he was right or wrong.

15. Imagery Practice with Magic Bag: Teacher Describes and Student Images and Guesses the Name

- Teacher feels inside the Magic Bag.
- Teacher feels, visualizes, and verbalizes.
- Teacher looks for signs that the student is imaging.
- Student guesses the name of the toy.
- Teacher gets the toy she described out of the bag and the student gets to see if he was right or wrong.

16. Imagery Practice with Magic Bag: Student Peeks Inside, Images, and Describes

- Student peeks inside the Magic Bag, choosing a toy to describe.

- Student describes the toy with details to help the teacher picture and guess the name of the toy.
- Teacher looks for signs that the student is imaging.
- Teacher describes what the student's words made her picture.
- Teacher guesses the name of the toy.
- Student gets the toy out of the bag to show the teacher if she is right or wrong.

Group Instruction

The biggest challenge in group instruction is keeping the attention of each student. Manage your group with the thumbs-up or thumbs-down gesture and reward students randomly for participating.

- Introduce the Picture Structure Words to a group, using the same steps as in individual instruction, making sure to get all the students involved. For example, when introducing *movement* and *color*, have the group participate in movements such as hopping around the room or have the group point out items of a particular color. Randomly, not round robin, encourage the whole group to respond with thumbs-up or thumbs-down to each student's response.

- In receptive and expressive practice with the picture cards, continue to keep the whole group participating and responding in turn. Ask one student to find one picture and the next to find another, while those students not directly involved respond with thumbs-up or thumbs-down gestures. This activity easily turns into a fun game that allows you to keep "score" of which students are able to identify and respond correctly to the picture cards.

  Picture Imagery practice is done cooperatively with one object shown to the whole group. Once all students have closed their eyes, each student gets a chance to say one thing about what they imaged.

  When you begin to work on vocabulary within categories, have the students take turns finding pictures that would fit into the chosen category.

In Expressive Practice and Imagery Practice with a picture vocabulary book, students take turns identifying and recalling objects within the category.

- The Magic Window steps need to be modified slightly for small or large group instruction. Have one student find and name the object in the window and let the other students use structure words to help describe it. Then have another student guide the window and name the next object. Likewise, the students should take turns using the Magic Glass, with one student identifying the part and others verbalizing its descriptive details. The thumbs-up or thumbs-down gesture keeps other students involved when one is taking a turn.

- The Magic Bag exercises are played like a guessing game. Students take turns feeling the objects in the bag and using the structure words to describe them while you and the others guess their identity. Imagery Practice is done in a similar manner. As you describe the object in the bag, the students take turns guessing what it is.

Summary: Step 4

Talking Sentences

Goal: To develop imagery and increase the complexity and length of sentences in expressive language.

1. Talking Two-Word Sentences with Teacher Generating the Change

- Teacher creates a sentence with a noun and a verb.
- Language is concretized on colored squares with toys or picture cards.
- Teacher changes one word at a time.
- Teacher starts with a noun on the first square and a Movement Card on the second square.
- Student touches each square and says sentence.
- Teacher changes a word.
- Student touches each square and says the sentence.
- Student changes the square or square and card, as appropriate.

2. Talking Two-Word Sentences with Student Generating the Change

- Student chooses an object and a Movement Card and places them on colored squares.
- Student touches each square and says the sentence.

- Student chooses a new object or Movement Card, changing one word in the sentence.
- Student changes the square or square and card, as appropriate.
- Student touches each square and says the sentence.

3. Talking Two-Word Sentences with Imagery for the Verb

- Teacher creates a two-word sentence without concretizing the verb with a Movement Card.
- Student pictures the verb.
- Teacher changes one word in the sentence.
- Student touches each square and says the sentence.
- Student may act out the verb and may take a turn making the changes in the sentence.
- A colored square changes when a word changes.

4. Talking Two-Word Sentences with Imagery for Whole Sentence

- Teacher creates a sentence without placing objects and cards on the squares.
- Student touches each square and says the sentence.
- Teacher encourages the student to picture.
- Teacher changes one word in the sentence.
- Student touches each square and says the sentence.
- Student may make the change and verbalize the sentence.

5. Adjectives for a Three-Word Sentence

- Teacher places a new square and adds an adjective before the noun in the sentence.
- Student touches each square and says the sentence.
- Teacher encourages the student to picture.
- The words may or may not be concretized on the sentence.

6. Concept Card for a Three-Word Sentence

- The Concept Card is used at the end of a sentence.
- Student chooses the Concept Card to put on a square.
- Student touches each square and says the sentence.
- Teacher or the student changes a word in the sentence.

7. Adding Articles and Connectors

- Student says a two-word sentence.
- Teacher places a new square to represent the article.
- Teacher prints the article on a 3x5 card to concretize the word but does not expect the student to read it.
- Student touches each square and says the sentence.
- Teacher or the student makes a change to the sentence by moving either the noun or the verb.
- Student touches each square and says the sentence.

8. Four- to Seven-Word Sentences

- Build sentences sequentially.
- Do not go beyond a seven-word sentence.
- May concretize a word at any time with an object or a card.

9. Talking Sentences for Prosody

- Teacher lines up the colored squares for a simple sentence.
- Teacher moves the first square up and says that word louder.
- Student says the sentence with the emphasized word.
- Teacher moves the first square down, moves the second up, and says the sentence with the new emphasis.
- Student says the sentence with the emphasized word.

- Teacher explains how saying a word loud makes that word's image the most important.

Group Instruction

Modify the Talking Sentences step with the varying skill levels of your students in mind. If there is a wide range in their levels of proficiency, you will need to have each student practice a sentence suitable for them, moving randomly from student to student. If their levels of ability are fairly close, then you can use one master sentence for the entire group, with you and the students both making changes to it. Call on each student randomly to change a single word, and then have the whole group participate by verbalizing the sentence together.

Summary: Step 5

Simple Picture to Picture

Goal: To develop verbalization from a given picture, using the Picture Structure Words for details to increase the length and complexity of expressive language.

1. Object to Picture

- Teacher presents two toys for the student to describe.
- Student chooses one toy he wants to describe, hiding it behind the Magic Door so the teacher can't see it.
- Student sees, feels, and describes the toy, using the structure words for details.
- Teacher questions to increase his verbalization, "Your words make me picture...." "What should I picture for ...?"
- Teacher guesses the toy.
- Student opens the Magic Door if teacher got it right.
- Teacher and the student discuss the parts she didn't picture.

2. Student and Teacher Describe a Picture

- Teacher and the student look at a simple picture.
- Teacher directs the description to the gestalt and then the details of the picture.
- Student touches and talks about specific parts, using structure words for details.

- Student may place a Magic Stone on the parts he describes.
- Teacher questions the student to increase his verbalization.
- Student may check through the structure words.
- Teacher and the student may take turns describing parts.
- Teacher helps the student summarize all they saw.

3. Imagery Practice After Picture Description

- Teacher and the student look again at the picture they have just described.
- Teacher hides the picture.
- Student describes his imagery.
- Teacher questions to direct his imagery, "What did you picture for...?"
- When the student has completed his verbalization, he sees the picture again.
- Teacher looks for signs the student is imaging.
- Teacher may take a turn and tell the student what she remembers to prompt his imagery.

4. Simple Picture to Picture

- Student hides a picture behind the Magic Door.
- Student describes the picture, using the structure words for detail.
- Teacher questions to increase his verbalization, "Your words make me picture...." "What should I picture for...?"
- Teacher gives a summary after the student has completed his description, "Your words made me picture...."
- Student opens the Magic Door and teacher sees the picture.
- Teacher and the student compare her imagery to the picture.
- Teacher says, "Great, I picture a...." "I didn't picture this...."

Group Instruction

The Simple Picture to Picture lessons are easily modified to accommodate the involvement of an entire group. In the Object to Picture little step and the Student and Teacher Describe a Picture little step, have the entire group look at the object/picture and then question random students to check their imagery, using the structure words to increase the detail of their descriptions. The entire group can build an image together in the Imagery Practice little step, and in the final Simple Picture to Picture step, the whole group can participate in describing the picture to the instructor. Remember to call on students randomly, ensuring that the entire group stays engaged and attentive.

Summary: Step 6

Simple Word Imaging

> **Goal:** The goal of this step is to develop visualization from the smallest unit of language—a word.

1. Word to Object to Imagery

- Teacher says a word and asks the student to picture the word and then find a toy to match the word.
- Student finds the toy, touching and feeling it to enhance his imagery.
- Teacher hides the toy and asks the student to picture it and tell her about it.
- Student verbalizes his imagery, using the structure words to aid in details.
- Teacher questions to extend the student's imagery.
- When the student's verbal description is complete, he may check through each structure word again, putting them to "sleep."
- Teacher gives a summary, "Your words made me picture…."
- Teacher and the student look at the toy again to check their imagery.
- The Magic Door can be used to hide the toy.

2. Word to Picture to Imagery

- Teacher says a word and asks the student to picture the word and then find a picture card to match the word.
- Student finds the card and looks at it carefully before the teacher hides it behind the Magic Door.
- Student verbalizes his imagery, using the structure words to aid in details.
- Teacher questions to extend the student's imagery.
- When the student's verbal description is complete, he may check through each structure word again, putting them to "sleep."
- Teacher gives a summary, "Your words made me picture...."
- Teacher and the student open the Magic Door and compare their imagery to the picture card.

3. Known Noun Imaging

- Teacher says a known noun and asks the student to picture it.
- Student verbalizes his imagery, using the structure words to aid in details.
- Teacher questions to extend the student's imagery.
- Teacher looks for signs that student is imaging.
- Teacher may take a turn visualizing.
- When the student's verbal description is complete, he may check through each structure word again, putting them to "sleep."
- Teacher gives a summary, "Your words made me picture...."

Group Instruction

In the Word to Object to Imagery and the Word to Picture to Imagery lessons, have the students take turns finding the items you describe. For the remainder of those lessons, and in the Known Noun Imaging lesson as well, call randomly on students in the group to give descriptions. Encourage students to respond nonverbally to the responses of their peers, with thumbs-up or thumbs-down gestures.

Summary: Step 7

Simple Sentence Imaging

Goal: The goal of this step is to develop visualizing and verbalizing for a single sentence.

1. Visualizing and Verbalizing a Simple Sentence

- Teacher creates a simple sentence using the known noun just visualized and verbalized in the Word Imaging step.
- Teacher questions with choice and contrast to help the student develop detailed, vivid imagery and verbalization.
- Student checks through the structure words after he has visualized and verbalized the sentence.
- He "wakes up" the structure words and reverbalizes his imagery.
- Teacher summarizes, "Your words made me picture...."
- Student may keep the structure words in front of him to assist his imaging.
- Use sound effects to assist in developing vivid imagery.

2. Using a Concept Card to Visualize and Verbalize a Phrase

- Teacher says a concept.
- Student finds the Concept Card.

- Teacher says an action involving the concept.
- Student performs the action and verbalizes it.

3. Visualizing and Verbalizing a Phrase

- Teacher says a phrase.
- Student pictures the phrase, then does the action and verbalizes it.

Group Instruction

The Simple Sentence Imaging lessons are done with a group of students in the same manner as they are with a single student. Read the sentence to the entire group and then, using the structure words to build detailed imagery, question random students on each structure word. Be sure to include and encourage gesturing in the lesson, as it helps all students in the group build the same image.

Summary: Step 8
Talking Picture Stories

Goal: The goal is to develop gestalt imagery from given pictures and extend expressive language into a story summary.

1. Sequencing Picture Stories

- Teacher checks to be sure the student has mastery of the concepts *first* and *last.*
- Teacher places Picture Sequence Cards in random order for the student to describe.
- Teacher questions to specific details to assist the student with the sequencing task.
- Student describes and places the sequence cards in order, from first to last.
- Student touches each sequence card to verbalize the story.
- Begin with two Picture Sequence Cards and extend up to five cards.

2. Visualizing and Verbalizing Picture Stories

- Teacher places Picture Sequence Cards in random order for the student to describe.
- Teacher questions to specific details to assist the student with the sequencing task.

- Student describes and places sequence cards in order from first to last.
- Student touches each sequence card to verbalize the story.
- Student puts the sequence cards to "sleep" by turning the cards over.
- Student touches each sequence card and reverbalizes the story sequence from his own imagery-recall.
- If needed, let the student peek at a card to trigger imagery and recall.
- Extend the talking picture stories lessons to four and five cards.

Group Instruction

As in previous steps, adapt Talking Picture Stories to a group by having the students work on the lesson together. Encourage the group to respond nonverbally to student responses, and question students randomly, to make sure all stay attentive and involved. When summarizing the picture story, have different students come forward to touch the cards and tell what happened next.

Summary: Step 9

Simple Sentence by Sentence

Goal: The goal is to begin to develop and verbally describe an imaged gestalt from simple, connected sentences.

1. **Simple Sentence by Sentence**

   - Teacher says a simple, high-imagery sentence to the student.
   - Student places a colored square on the table as an anchor for his sentence-imagery, and then visualizes and verbalizes the sentence.
   - The sentence has words student is familiar with, which may elicit sound effects to enhance imagery.
   - Teacher questions student's imagery with choice and contrast, keeping in mind the importance of questioning to the gestalt.
   - Teacher questions to the main character or concept first, and then to the familiar structure words.
   - Student may check through some of the Picture Structure Words to develop detailed imagery for each sentence.
   - Teacher says the next sentences and directs the student to form a gestalt with his imagery, not just separate, unrelated parts.
   - Student places colored squares for each sentence and then visualizes and verbalizes the sentence.

- Student goes through the two- to three-sentence paragraph sentence by sentence.
- Teacher touches each square and gives a picture summary by verbally describing the images the student created for each sentence. The student judges right or wrong.
- Teacher prompts the student to contribute to the picture summary by giving him imagery clues and pausing to help him recall and verbalize his imagery.
- Teacher collects the colored squares and together she and the student give a word summary by verbally summarizing the whole paragraph.

Group Instruction

Continue to engage the entire group as you visualize and verbalize each sentence by calling randomly on students to describe what they had imaged for each sentence, adding richness to the imagery. Continue to develop imagery through your questioning, and rephrase the student descriptions by saying, "Your words are making us picture...." Once each sentence is complete, you can have the group judge right or wrong with verbal or nonverbal responses. This practice helps close the circle for the students, and helps them apprehend the gestalt of the sentence.

Bibliography

Aristotle. (1972). *Aristotle on memory.* Providence, RI: Brown University Press.

Arnheim, R. (1966). Image and thought. In G. Kepes (Ed.). *Sign, image, symbol.* New York: George Braziller, Inc.

Arnheim, R. (1969). *Visual thinking.* Los Angeles, CA: University of California Press.

Beck, I. L. (2005). Proceedings of IDA '05: International Dyslexia Association Annual Conference.

Beck, I. L., & McKeown, M. G., & Kucan, L. (2002). *Bringing words to life: Robust vocabulary instruction.* New York: Guilford Press.

Bell, N. (1991). Gestalt imagery: A critical factor in language comprehension. *Annals of Dyslexia*, 41, 246-260.

Bell, N. (1991). *Visualizing and verbalizing for language comprehension and thinking.* Paso Robles, CA: Academy of Reading Publications.

Bell, N. (1997). *Seeing stars: Symbol imagery for phonemic awareness, sight words, and spelling.* San Luis Obispo, CA: Gander Publishing.

Bell, N. & Tuley, K. (1997). *On cloud nine: Visualizing and verbalizing for math.* San Luis Obispo, CA: Gander Publishing.

Bleasdale, F. (1983). Paivio's dual-coding model of meaning revisited. In J. C. Yuille (Ed.). *Imagery, memory and cognition: Essays in honor of Allan Paivio.* New Jersey: Lawrence Erlbaum Associates.

Boehm, A. E. (2001). *Boehm-3 preschool: Boehm test of basic concepts.* San Antonio, TX: Psychological Corp.

Bosshardt, H. G. (1975). The influence of visual and auditory images on visual and auditory word identification. *Psychological Research.*

Bower, G.H., & Morrow, D.G. (1990) Mental models in narrative comprehension. *Science*, 247(4938), 44-48.

Briggs, J. (1988). *Fire in the crucible: The alchemy of creative genius.* New York: St. Martin's Press.

Buzan, T. (1976). *Use both sides of your brain.* New York: E.D. Burton, New York.

Changeux, J. (1985). *Neuronal man: The biology of mind.* New York: Pantheon Books.

Clark, J. M., & Paivio, A. (1991). Dual coding theory and education. *Educational Psychology Review*, 3(3), 149-170.

Farah, M. J. (1984). The neurological basis of mental imagery: A componential analysis. *Cognition*, 18(1-3), 245-272.

Flowers, T. (1987). *Activities for developing pre-skill concepts in children with autism.* Austin, TX: PRO-ED.

Foley, M. A., & Wilder, A. (1989). *Developmental comparisons of the effects of type of imaginal elaboration on memory*. Paper read at the Biennial Meeting of the Society for Research in Child Development. Kansas City, MO.

Geschwind, N. (1974). *Selected papers on language and the brain.* Boston, MA.: D. Reidel Publishing.

Greenspan, S. & Lewis, N. B. (1999). *Building healthy minds: The six experiences that create intelligence and emotional growth in babies and young children.* Cambridge, MA.: Perseus Books.

Greenspan, S. & Salmon, J. (1995). *The challenging child: Understanding, raising, and enjoying the five "difficult" types of children.* Reading, MA.: Perseus Books.

Greenspan, S. & Shanker, S. G. (2004). *The first idea: How symbols, language, and intelligence evolved from our primate ancestors to modern humans.* Cambridge, MA.: Da Capo Press.

Greenspan, S. & Wieder, S. (1998). *The child with special needs: Encouraging intellectual and emotional growth.* Reading, MA.: Perseus Books.

Hanna, S. & Wilford, S. (1990). *Floor time: Tuning in to each child.* New York: Scholastic Inc.

Healy, J. M. (1990). *Endangered minds: Why our children don't think.* New York: Simon and Schuster.

Healy, J. M. (2004). *Your child's growing mind: Brain development and learning from birth to adolescence* (3rd ed.). New York: Broadway Books.

Horgan, J. (June 1991). Profile: Physicist John A. Wheeler. *Scientific American*, 36-37.

Interdisciplinary Council on Developmental & Learning Disorders (1997). *Approaches to developmental and learning disorders in infants and children: Theory & practice 1997.* Rockville, MD.

Interdisciplinary Council on Developmental & Learning Disorders (1999). Proceedings of ICDLD '99: *Third Annual International Conference: Autism and Disorders of Relating and Communicating.* McLean, VA.

Interdisciplinary Council on Developmental & Learning Disorders (2000). *Clinical practice guidelines: Redefining the standards of care for infants, children, and families with special needs.* Bethesda, MD.

James, W. (1950). *The principles of psychology: The famous long course complete and unabridged.* Mineola, NY: Dover Publications, Inc.

Katz, A. N., & Paivio, A. (1975) Imagery variables in concept identification. *Journal of Verbal Learning and Verbal Behavior*, 14(3), 284-293.

Kosslyn, S. M. (1975). Information representation in visual images. *Cognitive Psychology*, 7, 341-370.

Kosslyn, S. M. (1976). Using imagery to retrieve semantic information: A developmental study. *Child Development*, 47, 434-444.

Kosslyn, S. M. (1983). *Ghosts in the mind's machine.* New York: W.W. Norton.

Kosslyn, S. M. (1985). Stalking the mental image. *Psychology Today* 19, 23-28.

Kosslyn, S. M. (1994). *Image and brain: The resolution of the imagery debate.* Cambridge, MA: MIT Press.

Kosslyn, S. M. & Koenig, O. (1992). *Wet mind: The new cognitive neuroscience.* New York: The Free Press: A division of Macmillan, Inc.

Kwas, S. E. (Ill.) (2001). *Learning block books, 26 board books in a box!* Vancouver, BC: Chronicle Books.

La Bretesche, Geneviève de. (2005). *Scholastic first picture dictionary.* New York: Scholastic Inc.

Laughlin, C. D., & McManus, J., & d'Aquili, E. G. (1990). *Brain, symbol and experience.* Boston, MA.: Shambhala Publications, Inc.

Lindamood, P. & Lindamood, P. (1998) *The Lindamood phoneme sequencing program for reading, spelling, and speech* (3rd ed.). Austin, TX: PRO-ED.

Macht, M., & Scheirer, J. C. (1975). The effect of imagery on accessibility and availability in a short-term memory paradigm. *The Journal of Verbal Learning and Verbal Behavior,* 14(10).

Marks, D. F. (1972). Vividness of visual imagery and effect on function. In P. Sheehan (Ed.). *The Function and Nature of Imagery.* New York: Academic Press.

Morris, P. E., & Hampson, P. J. (1983). *Imagery and consciousness.* New York: Academic Press.

Murphy, C. (2001). *Slide 'n' seek opposites.* New York: Little Simon.

Paivio, A. (1969) Mental imagery in associative learning and memory. *Psychological Review,* 76, 241-263.

Paivio, A. (1971). *Imagery and verbal processes.* New York: Holt, Rinehart, and Winston. Reprinted 1979. Hillsdale New Jersey: Lawrence Erlbaum Associates.

Paivio, A. (1986). *Mental representations: A dual coding approach.* New York: Oxford University Press.

Paivio, A. (1996). *Proceedings of LBRT '96: Presentation at the National Lindamood-Bell Research and Training Conference.* San Francisco, CA.

Piaget, J., & Barbel, I. (1969). *The psychology of the child.* New York: Basic Books, Inc.

Piaget, J., & Inhelder, B. (1971). *Imagery and the child.* New York: Basic Books, Inc.

Pietsch, P. (1975). The optics of memory. *Harpers,* 251(1507).

Pressley, G. M. (1976). Mental imagery helps eight year olds remember what they read. *Journal of Educational Psychology,* 68, 355-359.

Pribram, K. H. (1971). *Languages of the brain: Experimental paradoxes and principles in neuropsychology.* New York: Brandon House, Inc.

Pribram, K. H. (1991). *Brain and perception: Holonomy and structure in figural processing.* Hillsdale, NJ: Erlbaum.

Priddy, R. (2002). *My big animal book.* New York: St. Martin's Press.

Priddy, R. (2004). *My little word book.* New York: Priddy Books.

Richardson, A. (1969). *Mental imagery.* London: Routledge & Kegan Paul.

Rollins, M. (1989). *Mental imagery: On the limits of cognitive science.* New Haven, CT: Yale University Press.

Sadoski, M. (1983). An exploratory study of the relationship between reported imagery and the comprehension and recall of a story. *Reading Research Quarterly*, 19(1), 110-123.

Sadoski, M. (1985). The natural use of imagery in story comprehension and recall: Replication and extension. *Reading Research Quarterly*, 20(5), 658-667.

Sadoski, M., & Goetz, E. T., & Kangiser, S. (1988). Imagination in story response: Relationships between imagery, affect, and structural importance. *Reading Research Quarterly*, 23(3), 320-336.

Sadoski, M., & Goetz, E.T., & Olivarez, A., & Lee, S., & Roberts, N. M. (1990). Imagination in story reading: The role of imagery, verbal recall, story analysis, and processing levels. *Journal of Reading Behavior*, 22(1), 55-70.

Sadoski, M., & Quast, Z. (1990). Reading response and long-term recall for journalistic text: The roles of imagery, affect, and importance. *Reading Research Quarterly*, 25(3).

Samples, R. E. (1975). Learning with the whole brain. *Human Behavior.*

Samuels, M. & N. (1975). *Seeing with the mind's eye.* New York: Random House.

Sheehan, P.W. (Ed.) (1972). *The function and nature of imagery.* New York: Academic Press.

Simon, H. A. (1972). What is visual imagery? An information processing interpretation. In L.W. Gregg (Ed.). *Cognition in Learning and Memory.* New York: John Wiley & Sons, Inc.

Smith, B.D., & Stahl, N., & Neil, J. (1987). The effect of imagery instruction on vocabulary development. *Journal of College Reading and Learning*, 20, 131-137.

Stages® Learning Materials. (2004). *Language builder picture cards.* Chico, CA: Author.

Tarnish, R. (2002). *First concepts numbers.* New York: St. Martin's Press.

Twachtman-Cullen, D. (1998). *Maximizing the effectiveness of socio-communicative interactions in more able verbal children.* Paper read at the Child with Special Needs, Autism Preconference, Anaheim, CA, April.

Untermeyer, L. (1959). *The golden treasury of poetry.* New York: Golden Press.

Wepman, J. M. (1976). Aphasia: Language without thought or thought without language? *ASHA, 18*(3), 131-136.

Whittington, M. (2002). *First concepts opposites.* New York: St. Martin's Press.

Wittrock, M. C. *The generative processes of memory.* Manuscript from Education Department at University of California, Los Angeles.